THE IRISH HARP BOOK

A Tutor and Companion

THE IRISH HARP BOOK

A Tutor and Companion

SHEILA LARCHET CUTHBERT

Including works by the following:

The Harper-Composers

17th-19th Century Irish Composers

Contemporary Irish Composers
(work for this volume commissioned by Cairde na Cruite)

Facsimile Edition

CARYSFORT PRESS

Dublin

CARYSFORT PRESS LIMITED

58 Woodfield
Scholarstown Road
Dublin 16

THE IRISH HARP BOOK – A Tutor and Companion

ISBN 1-904505-08-2

Note:

The Irish Harp Book incorporates *Tutor for the Irish Harp* and *27 Studies* by the late Mother Attracta Coffey, Loreto Abbey, Rathfarnham.

[First published in 1975 by Mercier Press
Reprinted in 1977
Reprinted in 1985
Reprinted in 1993]

Facsimile Edition 2004

Printed in the Republic of Ireland by Eprint

PREFACE

The Irish Harp Book was first published in 1975, almost thirty years ago. At that time, it was my hope that its publication would mark the beginning of a new and exciting era for the harp. In the intervening years, it has been gratifying to witness the growth of interest, as new generations of players develop and perfect their own styles of playing, while at the same time continuing to learn and pass on traditional tunes. The harp is indeed enjoying an unprecedented level of recognition and interest.

I wish to extend my deepest gratitude to those who helped to make *The Irish Harp Book* a reality: the late Eibhlín Ní Chathailriabhaigh, founder-member and former President of Cairde na Cruite, the Mother Superior (at the time) of Loreto Abbey, Rathfarnham, and the late Dr Donal O'Sullivan, all of whom showed great generosity in giving me unconditionally the use of so much music. Thanks are also due, of course, to our contemporary composers, whose works are being so widely performed.

To Gráinne and Micheál Yeats, two special friends, we owe our deep gratitude: their prodigious generosity has helped to make this reprinting possible. Also much appreciated are a number of donations from members and friends of Cairde na Cruite which helped to defray some of the printing costs.

May I again wish you many happy hours of music-making.

'Go raibh rath ar ár gcuid oibre.'

SHEILA LARCHET CUTHBERT
Dublin, 2004

Dedication

TO MY DEAR PARENTS

JOHN AND MADELEINE LARCHET

In grateful and loving memory

FOREWORD

What better way to introduce *The Irish Harp Book* to the student than by calling to mind the description by Giraldus Cambrensis of the performance of the Irish harpers in the twelfth century. His words have been used in praise and defence of our music so often that it would be ungracious to omit his name from a work of this kind. Besides, they are of relevance at least on this occasion. What impressed Giraldus Cambrensis when listening to these musicians was the rapidity of their playing, the unfailing accuracy of their finger work and yet the overall sweetness of their performance. He expressed no surprise at the type of music played, so that it is not rash to infer that what he heard was such as he was accustomed to listening to in those centres of learning and sophistication which he frequented on the Continent.

We are right to be pleased by these words of praise of Cambrensis. It is encouraging to know we belong to a musical people, for some peoples are more musical than others. But far too many people associated with music-making in Ireland behave as if it were purely a gift to be acquired overnight. Excellence at music demands long and arduous training, and the harpers whose performance so excited Cambrensis were highly-trained artists who owed their skill no less to their training than to their innate musical gifts. The student who seriously wishes to learn the harp will not be put off, then, if, at first sight, this tutor looks difficult or complicated. Rather will he be grateful that the author has been at such pains to provide so readily for him the means essential for realizing his ambition.

If a lengthy period of training is demanded of the student, he is not asked to await its completion before being permitted to enjoy the pleasure of playing real music. Almost immediately he meets with one of our oldest surviving melodies, *Cailín ó Chois tSiúire Mé*, a song air of the 16th century, preserved for us by its notation in manuscript collections of that century. As he progresses in his study he becomes acquainted with the compositions of Carolan and other harpers and with the folk airs which formed so large a part of the repertoire of the 18th century harpers, made familiar to us by the labours of Edward Bunting. The score or so of these melodies presented in this tutor are the merest sampling of a veritable treasure of music, a national store which contains literally thousands of melodies of the most diverse character and tonality, and spanning in time four centuries of musical history.

It will be of use, I think, to include in this introduction a very brief account of the harp in Irish history. It will recall to the Irish students the past glories of the instrument and be a source of enlightenment to the many overseas students who now eagerly await the advent of this tutor. It will, I hope, encourage both to sustain their efforts towards the mastery of it.

It is scarcely possible to exaggerate the esteem in which the harp was held in ancient Ireland. It is associated with the very origins of music in our oldest myths and legends. To it alone was properly attributed the three mystical feats of music-making: the *suantraí*, which threw all who heard it into the deepest slumber; the *geantraí*, which made the company irresistibly merry; and the *goltraí*, which plunged an audience into the deepest sorrow. The instrument and the performer were deemed worthy subjects for his art by the *file* or professional poet; the obituaries of noted players were also worthy of notation by the native annalists. First introduced on the coinage in the middle of the sixteenth century, it is now the national emblem of the country. In its modern triangular form – which may indeed have been developed by Irish harpers – and in its earlier prototypes, the instrument has a history stretching well over a thousand years on this island.

The traditional manner of playing the Irish harp was lost when the last of the old Irish harpers passed away in the opening decades of the nineteenth century. That tradition cannot be revived, but any live tradition is no more than a body of practices and techniques which had a beginning at some point of time in the past and has been acted upon and moulded in its transmission to the present by a cohesive body of practitioners. The present cultivation of the Irish harp has been sustained too long to be dismissed as an ephemeral interest in things of the past. It is not fanciful, then, to see in it a nucleus from which will develop a national school of harping with a distinctively national style. Here it is encouraging to call to mind that a high accomplishment in the then modern music was part of the art of the Irish harpers when they were considered by Cambrensis to be the first of all nations. An intensive study of the harp music which has survived a teasing of the accounts of the manner of playing left by Bunting and other writers, and a critical examination of all the literary references, however vague, in Irish and in English, will surely shed some rays of light on the techniques and attitudes of the native harpers. The absorption of the results of such studies by a body of musicians, trained seriously and systematically, must inevitably tend towards the development of styles and techniques appropriate to the music and the instrument. It is heartening to know that studies of the kind have already been initiated by some of the contributors to this tutor.

In Ireland, as elsewhere, one senses a latent antagonism between 'art' and folk music. The contemptuous dismissal on the one hand and the declaration of total indifference on the other are signs of this phenomenon which, for reasons grounded in history, is more marked here, perhaps, than in other countries. Sheila Larchet Cuthbert, by persuading composers of the first rank in Ireland to compose works especially for her tutor and by her use of the older native music, must, whether by design or otherwise, achieve a considerable advance towards breaching that barrier between 'art' and folk music in Ireland. This would be not least among the many good results one may expect to flow from *The Irish Harp Book.*

I am grateful to *Cairde na Cruite* for their invitation to write this foreword – thus enabling me to be associated with the publication of *The Irish Harp Book* – and I look forward with confidence to the realisation of the author's hopes that this work will inaugurate a new and exciting era for our national instrument.

Breandán Breathnach
17 March, 1975

Contents

Parts of the Harp

(The Neo-Irish Model)

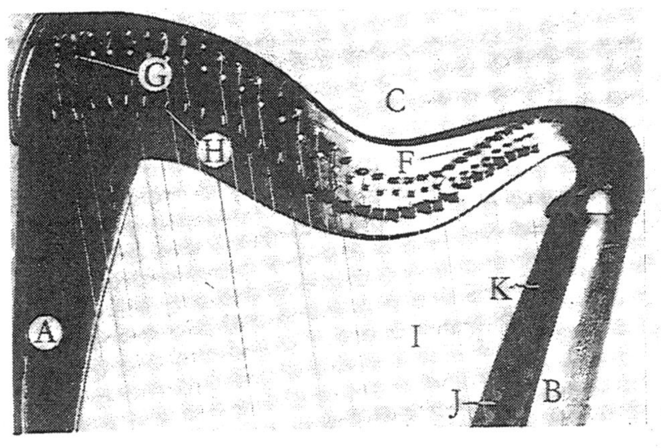

A. Forepillar (Lámhchrann)

B. Body (Com)

C. Curving Neck, or Harmonic Curve (An Mhuin)

D. Sounding Board (Fuaimchlár)

E. Feet (Cosa)

F. Tuning Pins (Bioráin Tiúnta)

G. Rest Pins (Bioráin Taca)

H. Blades (Lanna)

I. Strings (Téada)

J. Pegs (Pionnaí)

K. Eyelets (Súile)

L. Tuning Key (Eochair Thiúnta)

L

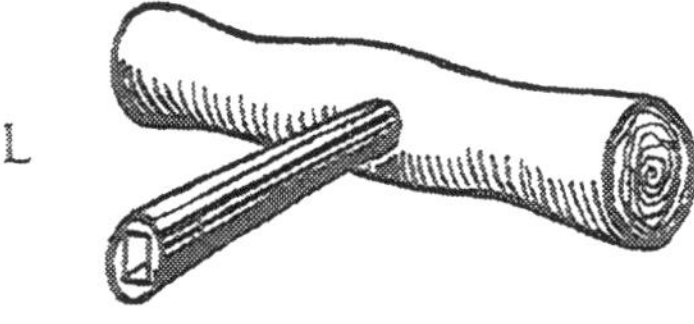

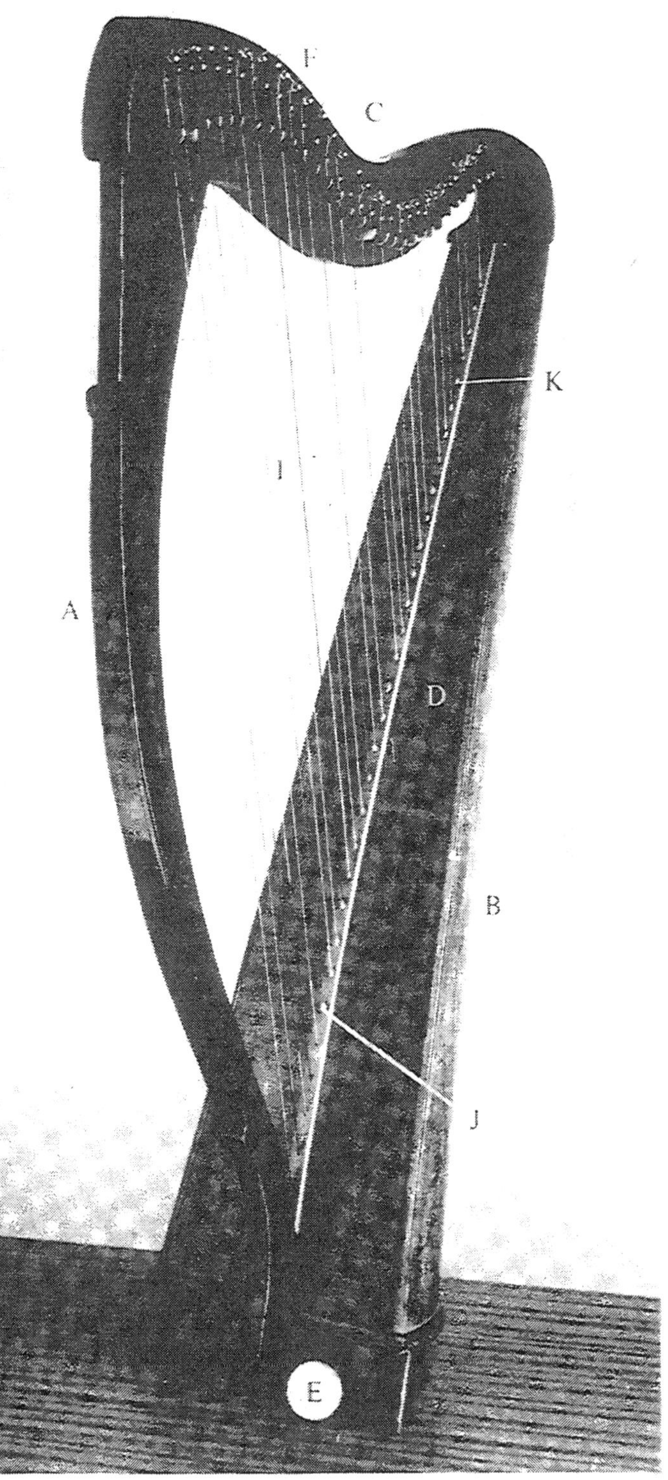

The harp shown here is by
Daniel Quinn of Dublin.
Pictures by Colman Doyle.

FIRST LESSON

The Instrument

THE COMPASS of the Irish Harp is usually four octaves with one or two additional notes at either end of the range making some 30 strings in all. The ideal compass is from E flat, first line below the bass stave to G, fourth line above the treble stave.

THE STRINGS are of catgut, except the four lowest ones which are of silver wire to render them more sonorous. To assist the eye in finding certain fixed points among so many strings, C's are coloured red and F's are green or black. Nylon strings are also in use.

TUNING The Harp is tuned in the Diatonic Scale of E flat major:

Every string can be raised one semitone by turning a Blade (or lever) at the top of the harp. One half turn upwards is sufficient to deflect the string and shorten its length. However, all the blades are in the neutral position (i.e. disengaged) when the harp is in the basic key of E flat major.

To facilitate those who may not be, as yet, acquainted with this key, it is proposed to tune the harp in the more familiar key of C major:

Firstly, engage each B, E and A Blade with its string, thereby producing B, E and A natural throughout the entire compass of the harp.

Using a C tuning fork, begin from middle C and set one octave upwards, proving the correctness of the tuned notes with other consonant intervals. The following example shows the usual manner of tuning and proving.

Having set this octave "in intervals", it is now possible to tune the other strings "in octaves" from each note of this proven scale:

Thus:  etc. *

Because of the fundamental problem inherent in the "Equal-Tempered Scale", never tune the harp in octaves initially. They may be in tune with each other but the entire instrument will be out of tune.

It is impossible to stress sufficiently the importance of having a well-tuned harp. No playing, however good, can compensate for the omission of this primary necessity.

On the following page it will be seen how the complete range of 13 keys can be achieved by use of the other Blades but it is important to note that the mechanism has only a Single-Action to raise a semitone and cannot lower a string beneath its original pitch. Hence the key-limitation of the Irish Harp.*

It should be noted that while manipulating the Blades, a half turn towards the player is sufficient to raise the string, care should be taken when lowering the string, to turn the blade back again the way it came, i.e. down and away from the player into the neutral position, otherwise jarring noises against the strings may be produced.

As a Harpist is obliged to "make" his or her own key, the signature should be noted and the necessary blades altered. The left hand makes this adjustment as the mechanism is on that side of the Harp. In this Tutor, accidentals will be anticipated by writing, for example - C♯(3) - (i.e. C sharp in the 3rd octave from the top) at such a point as to allow time to turn the blade raising the string in question.

The manner of placing the instrument differs according to the particular model, the heavier old instruments being easier to play (especially if singing) when sitting to the left side of the Harp. The present lighter models require to be placed on a suitably built stool to bring them up to the correct playing level or if standing the Harp on the floor, it should be played from a low chair. In both cases the player should sit towards the edge of the chair, keeping the back straight. The first of these two methods is much the more practical but whatever the manner of placing the instrument, the following few points should be observed: The Harp should rest on its two hind feet, the two front ones being raised off the floor. It should be so balanced as to rest lightly against the right shoulder and should be gripped between the knees, thus giving the maximum control. If sitting to the side of the Harp, the player should sit well forward and as close as possible to the instrument. If using a stool it is advisable to cover the top with felt or baize to prevent the Harp from slipping.

* The deflection of a string by a blade shortens its vibrating length and so raises the pitch. As a consequence, the tone of the string is slightly affected. This is one of the reasons why E flat major has been chosen as the basic key, thus giving the most useful selection of nearly-related keys and avoiding as many sharp keys as possible. Consideration has also been given to the suitability of these keys for most voices.

The following illustrations should prove a helpful reference until the key-board and key-change system are thoroughly understood.

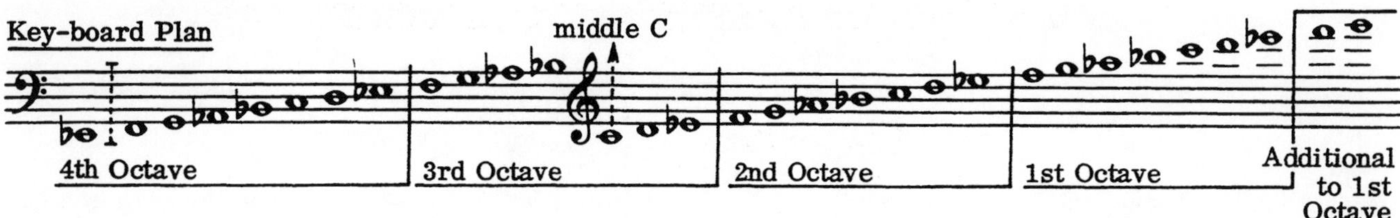

BLADES are named as E♭(1), F♯(2), C♮(3) etc. according to their register. Key Settings or Accidentals are prepared by these indications.

Range of all possible keys: 13 Major; 5 Relative Minor.

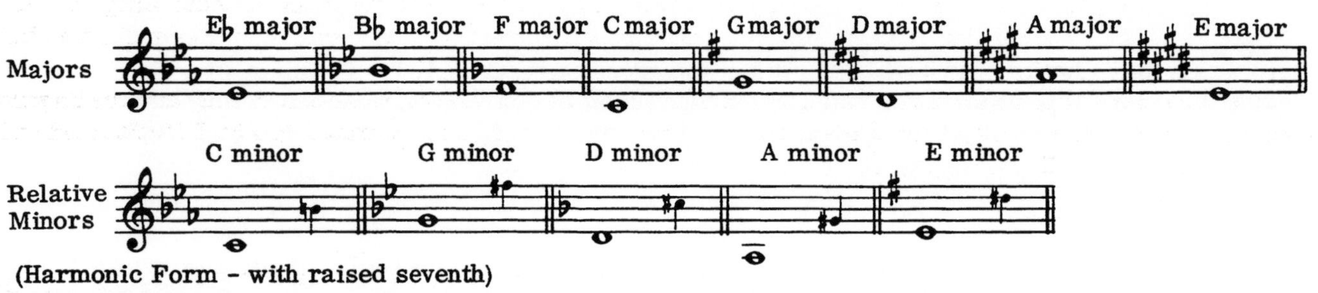

The various Blade positions when tuning in the full range of keys:

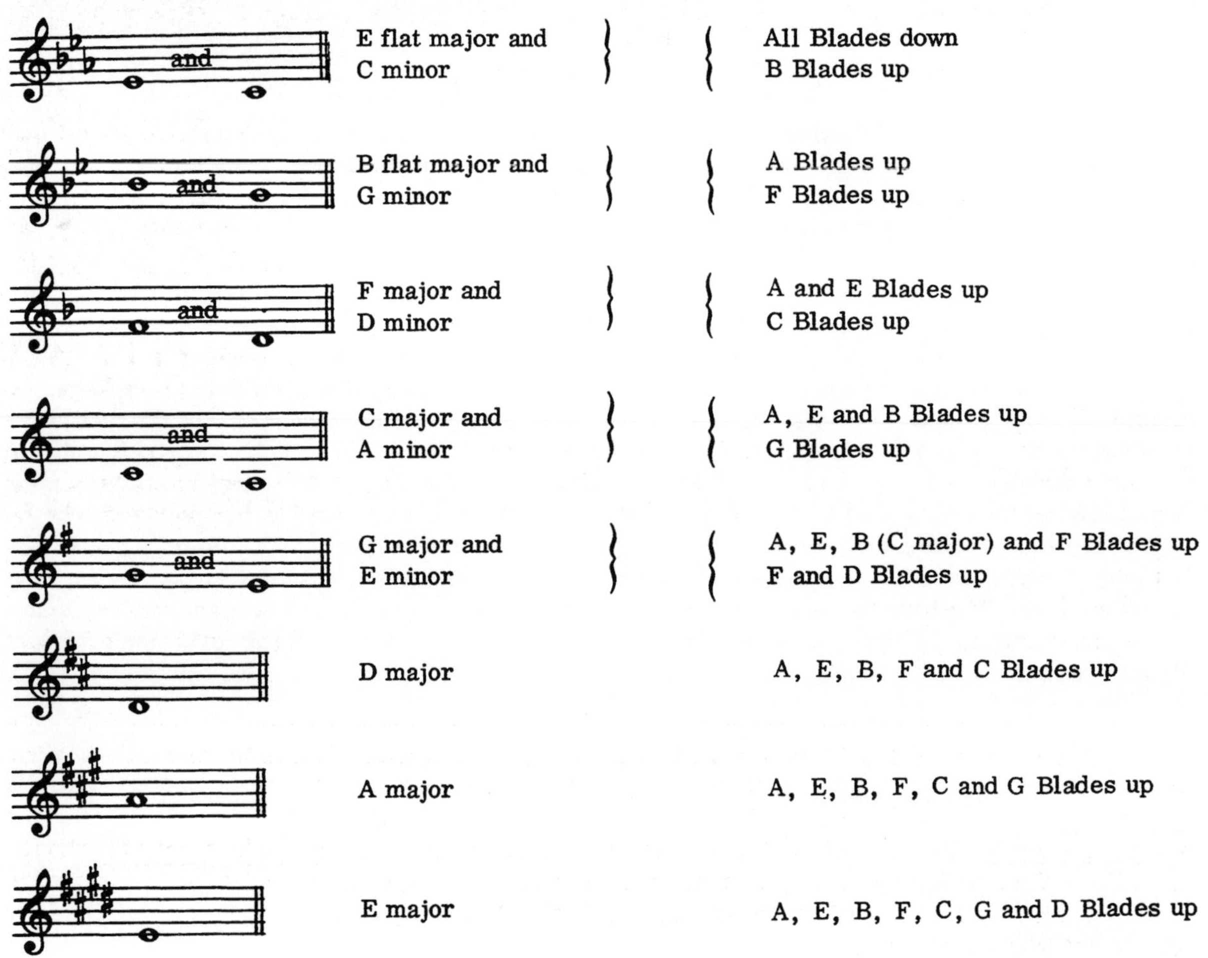

LESSON I

Position of Hands
First Simple Exercises and Studies
Fingering
First Simple Pieces

Eibhlín a Rún
Cailín ó Chois tSiúire Mé
Caoine Phiarais Feiritéir

POSITION OF THE HANDS

"Tone on the Harp is produced as much by the mind as by the fingers" an eminent Harpist once stated. Quality of tone, the first essential of harp playing, does indeed depend on this co-ordination but the initial requirement must be the position of the hands.

To obtain a full and beautiful tone, the thumbs should be placed high, without straining and the fingers extended, the wrist being slightly advanced towards the strings, as illustrated in Fig. I Right Hand and Fig. II Left Hand. The little finger is never used.

Fig. I

Fig. II

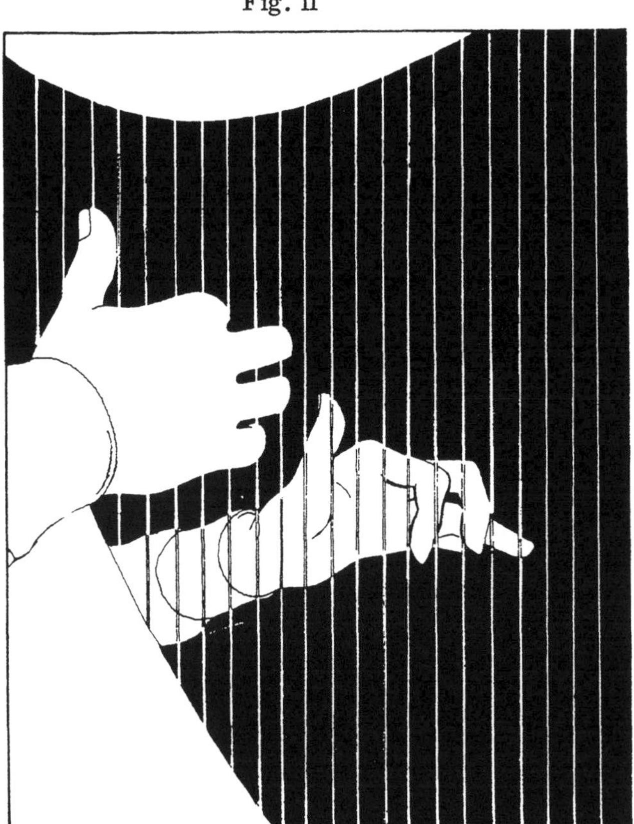

The position of the Right and Left Arms do not correspond. There is generally a point of contact between the Right Arm or Wrist and the Harp, depending on the register in which the Harpist is playing. In the lower octave the arm, midway between wrist and elbow, rests against the side of the instrument. As the hand ascends, the point of contact moves towards the wrist, while in the high register the hand or even the ball of the thumb may rest against the instrument. But the arm and elbow should always be on a level with the wrist. It is important to note that while the right arm, wrist or hand rests against the harp, it should not lean heavily on it.

The left arm should, like the right, be on a level with the wrist but it has no point of contact with the instrument at all; nor should the elbow be kept too close to the body.

The manner of plucking the strings is of great importance. The finger, on releasing the string should travel inwards to the palm of the hand and make contact with it. This complete finger action is essential. The thumb travels to the side of the first finger and makes contact with it.

The completed action of fingers and thumb is vital if the performer is to produce not only a full and beautiful tone but Resonance as well. When it is remembered that we are playing on an instrument almost entirely lacking in this latter commodity, the importance of good finger-control will be quickly realised.

Preparation of Fingers. This most important point consists of placing firmly one or more strings prior to the action of releasing the strings. The finger or thumb then travels rapidly to complete the action already referred to. The advantage of this preparation will be more fully appreciated later on when a succession of notes has to be played. It will also be found that the tone is improved by the steadying of the hand brought about by this preparation. But even in the playing of a single finger not linked with any other, the finger action procedure should be completed as before.

Try these first three simple Exercises with the Right Hand, placing the first finger and thumb together, holding down the thumb while the finger plays and after the thumb has played, placing both again on the next two notes and so on. Make sure to feel the contact of the first finger as it reaches the palm of the hand and the thumb as it falls onto the side of the first finger.

Throughout this Tutor the standard (universal) fingering will be used and the fingers numbered as follows:

Thumb	1st Finger	2nd Finger	3rd Finger
1	2	3	4

To have the assistance of the Colour guide on the keyboard, turn up the B, E and A Blades throughout, making these strings naturals from flats, thus putting the Harp into the key of C major. Remember the C strings are red and the F's are green (or black).

EXERCISE I

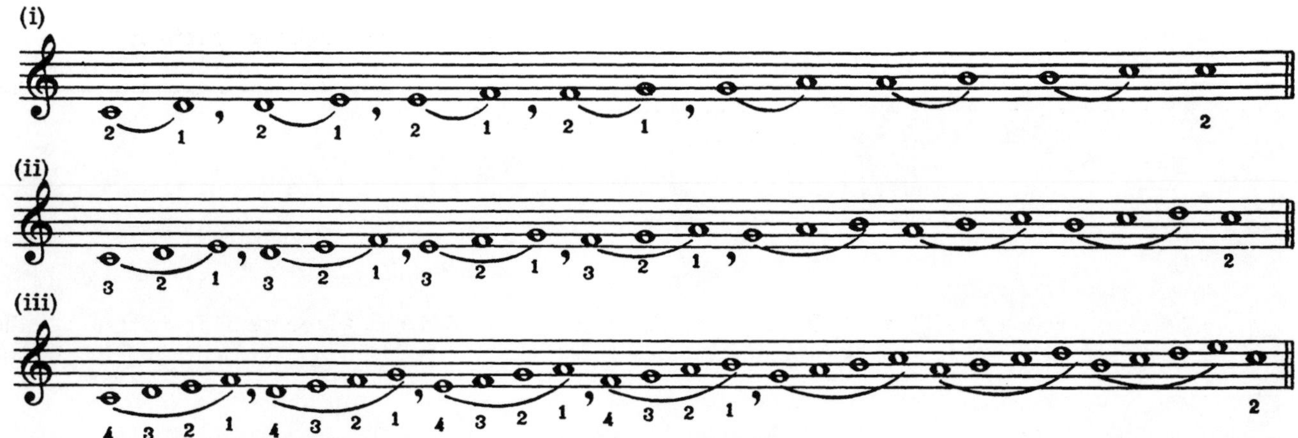

Try the same Exercises with the left hand, one octave lower.

IMPORTANT. As the fingers are quite unaccustomed to being "worked" in this manner, (i.e. being drawn rapidly into the palm of the hand), have patience in practising and never try to force this action by stiffening the hand or arm. On the contrary, try to be as relaxed as possible; the fingers will gain strength in time. The left hand has the harder task in plucking the heavier strings, especially the 4th finger, so "Festina Lente"! (hasten slowly.)

Because of the inherent lack of Resonance (as distinct from Vibration) in the instrument, it will be seen that we are nearly always occupied with "preparing" or "placing" fingers. It is only by this means that we can produce a LEGATO* sound so essential for good phrasing and the carrying of a melodic line - one of the most difficult aspects of harp playing.

Although no fingering can be said to be "absolute" because the musical text, phrasing, etc. dictates this to a great extent, the following rules could be described as "general", always allowing for flexibility should the musical sense require it:

Fingering of Intervals:

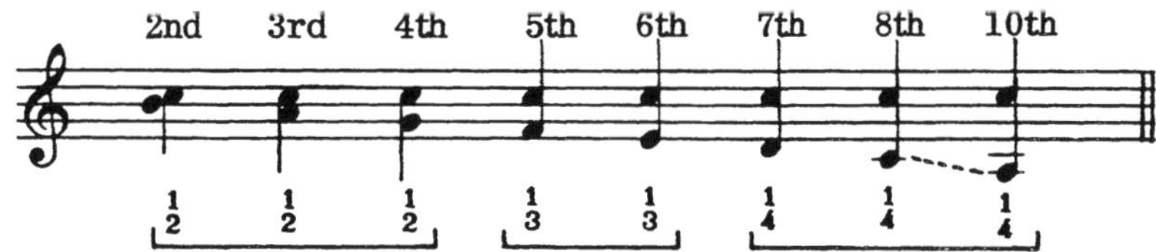

This fingering applies to both hands, of course.

Remember the following indications:

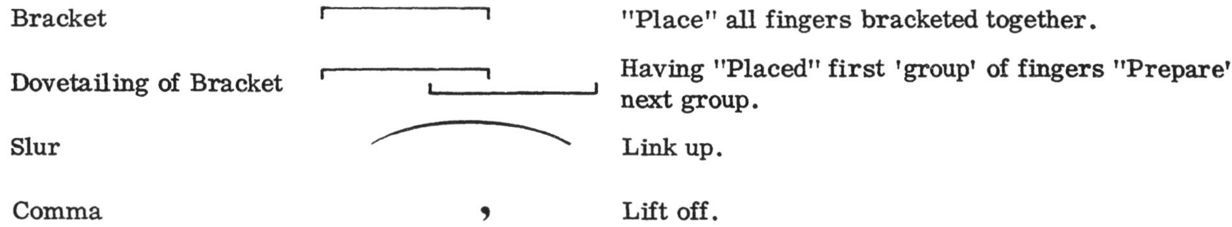

Bracket — "Place" all fingers bracketed together.

Dovetailing of Bracket — Having "Placed" first 'group' of fingers "Prepare" next group.

Slur — Link up.

Comma , — Lift off.

Position of Feet. If you are holding the Harp between the knees, place your feet firmly on the floor. They help to stabilise and control the instrument. Never try to play with the Harp resting against the knee.

*legato = connected

EXERCISE II (In C major)

Place firmly the four adjacent strings and continue to hold three throughout each exercise. Replace the finger being played on the 'rest' and count the four beats in order to time the replacement correctly.

R.H.

Continue with the left hand in the same manner.

L.H.

EXERCISE III (Continue in C major)

Throughout this Tutor a bracket ⌐¬ or slur ⌒ will be used, under or over the notes to indicate "placing" or "preparing" of fingers. Continue the following exercise making sure to observe correct finger action by plucking into the palm of the hand and by holding or releasing fingers as indicated:

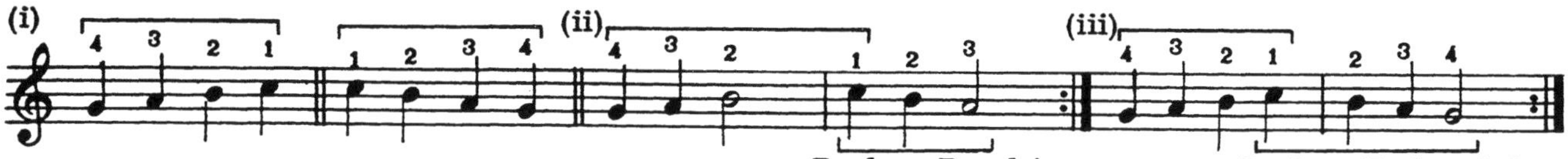

(i) (ii) (iii)

Replace B and A before releasing C.

Replace B, A and G before releasing C.

(iv)

comma = lift off hand

Continue with left hand, paying attention to the same details.

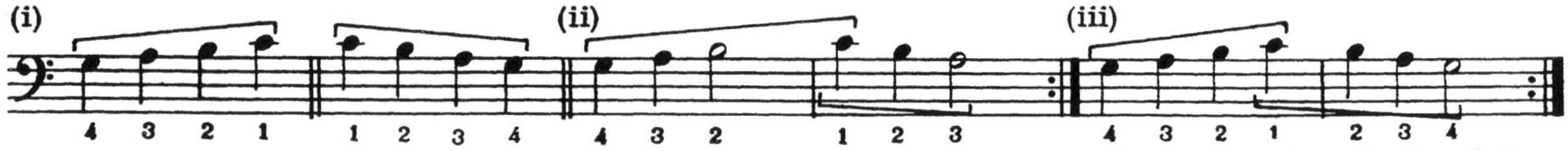

(i) (ii) (iii)

Replace B and A before releasing C.

Replace B, A and G before releasing C.

(iv)

comma = lift off hand

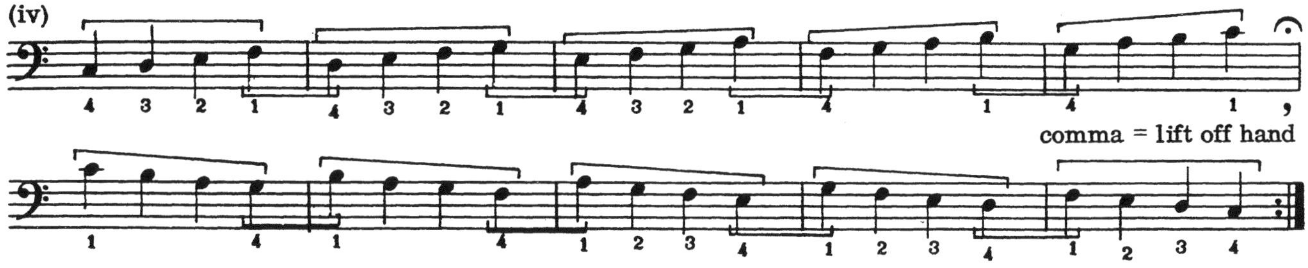

Practise all these Exercises, hands together too.

(v)

STUDIES

1. R.H.

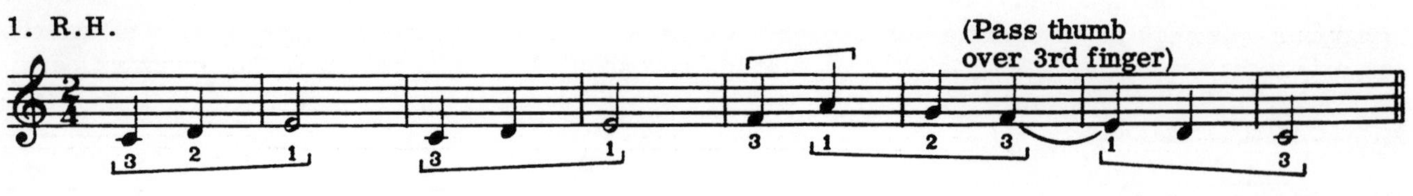

2. L.H.

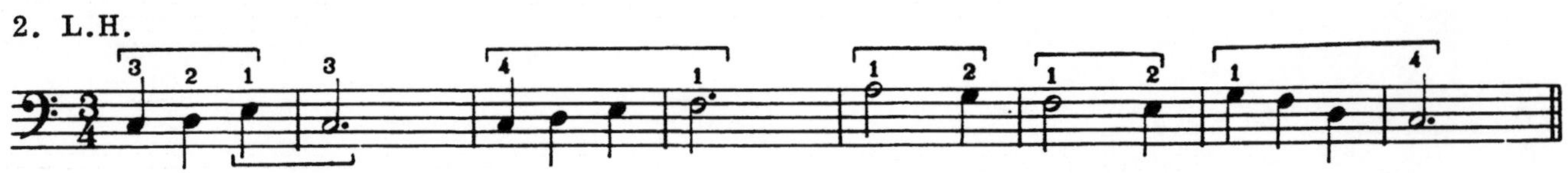

3.

PIECES

EIBHLÍN A RÚN

EIBHLÍN A RÚN - described as the queen of Irish love songs. Tradition ascribes it to the early 17th century poet, Carrol O'Daly.

Put the Harp into the basic key of E flat major by turning down all B, E and A Blades to their original positions (i.e. from ♮'s to ♭'s) (See Keyboard Plan on page 16).

CAILÍN Ó CHOIS tSIÚIRE MÉ

CAILÍN Ó CHOIS tSIÚIRE MÉ - Oldest tune extant.
Play the four 4-bar phrases as smoothly and simply as possible. The lines (¦) are merely to indicate phrasing.

CAOINE PHIARAIS FEIRITÉIR Slowly and sadly

CAOINE PIARAS FEIRITÉIR (A lament). Piaras Feiritéir - a country gentleman and man of letters resisted Cromwellian Forces in Kerry and was hanged by them in Killarney in 1657.

LESSON II

Explanation
Exercises
Scale and Arpeggio - E FLAT MAJOR
Study No.1
Pieces

Tiarna Mhaigh Eó
(David Murphy)
The Parting of Friends
(Bunting - Milligan Fox)

In the preceding lesson, we were introduced to the initial ways of using the fingers which produce certain desired results. e.g. ⌐¬ , ⌐¬ ∟⌟, ⌒ and , . A first attempt at the playing of "chords" was hinted at, (i.e. two or even three easily-placed notes to be played together) and all these points will be developed in the following lessons. But it is well to remember that Position and Complete Finger Action are the basic requirements on which to build the TECHNIQUE we need to play the harp.

The passing of the thumb over the other fingers or the passing of any one of the fingers under the thumb, is the means by which we move smoothly from one position to another and leads ultimately to the playing of a SCALE. A preliminary exercise will introduce this.

Try to keep the correct hand and thumb position. (See Figs. I and II on page 17) and complete the finger action, i.e. pull the fingers into the palm of the hand. This applies whether you pluck a single string, two or more together or several successive strings. Also observe your own position very carefully. Make sure that you sit up straight and towards the edge of the chair, with your feet placed firmly on either side of the Harp which should be gripped by the knees and resting against not leaning on the right shoulder. A good test of the correctness of your position is to lean slightly backwards from the Harp. If it is really properly balanced (i.e. gripped by your knees) it should remain upright; if it leans back with you, then you are not in control of it and this incorrect position will prove a hindrance to your finger technique. Angle the Harp slightly on your shoulder in order to see the whole keyboard at a glance without having to lean to the left side in order to see the top octave. This would be a defect in position.

More "continuity" in playing is now being introduced. It is important, therefore, that the fingers are "placed" and "prepared" properly. If 2, 3 or 4 are bracketed together, put them on the strings together. Do not allow them to "straggle" on. This would impede the style of playing required in Ex.vii, for example. For difference between "placing" and "preparing" see Ex.ii onwards.

INDEPENDENCE OF FINGERING and
EQUALITY OF TONE

One leads to the other and we are working to achieve both. Each finger must be made equally strong otherwise the "weak" one will let us down and notes will be poorly played or missed out.

Concentrate on equality of tone between the fingers especially during the playing of scales and arpeggios. It is easier to listen when we do not have to read music as well. Look at your fingers instead.

If we train the fingers correctly from the outset, they will eventually work as we want them to, almost automatically. But of course, our playing must never become like this!

EXERCISES

Practise this exercise very slowly, paying particular attention to equality of tone in all **fingers.** Notice how the hand "pivots" on the 4th finger as it turns underneath. Do not let the **fingers "straggle"** on if bracketed together.

(i)

SCALE and ARPEGGIO of E flat major

Make sure not to release thumb at top of scale until you have replaced the three other fingers for the descent. Otherwise there will be a break in continuity.

Practise all Exercises hands separately first and then together.

(iv)

(v)

(vi)

While practising the following Exercise, count aloud in order to "time" the replacement of the fingers. There should be no break in the continuity.

(vii)

Study No.1

VINER

*Allegretto = Rather lively

Tiarna Mhaigh Eó

Arranged by
Sheila Larchet-Cuthbert

DAVID MURPHY

TIARNA MHAIGH EÓ - Composed about the year 1717 by David Murphy, harper to Lord Mayo.

Allargando = Enlarging i.e. getting slower and fuller in tone.

The Parting of Friends (Na Cumainn)

From arrangement by
C. Milligan Fox

An example of a melody preserved by
HEMPSON (1695–1807)

THE PARTING OF FRIENDS - NA CUMAINN. A beautiful and melancholy air which harpers were accustomed to play at the end of a banquet or festival. Denis Hempson was an exponent of the most ancient style of playing and "THE PARTING OF FRIENDS" may be pointed to as an example of a melody preserved by him. Hempson was a performer, not a composer.

Adagio = Slow

Poco a poco = little by little.

LESSON III

Chord Playing
Exercises
Scales - B FLAT & F MAJOR
Studies Nos. 2 & 3
Pieces

The Irish Ho-hone
(Fitzwilliam Virginal Book)
Scarúint na gCompánach
(Rory Dall Ó Catháin)

CHORD PLAYING. There are three ways of playing chords on the Harp:

(i) Sec(1) or Dry (i.e.) all notes played exactly together.

(ii) Arpeggiando(2) (i.e.) all notes slowly opened out.

(iii) Effleurez(3) (i.e.) a "compromise" between the two.

This third manner of playing is by far the more widely used as the other two methods, while useful in making an occasional "effect", could become monotonous and even out of context; the first being too dull; the second unrhythmic. The French word "effleurez" (caress) is difficult to translate into our terms of reference but it gives to harp playing the uniquely liquid sound, so characteristic of this most lyrical instrument.

Technically speaking "effleurez" is arrived at by pulling the fingers very rapidly (into the palm of the hand, as always) thereby making the strings "speak" quickly and evenly. Naturally, this kind of ARTICULATION requires time and patience and will only be achieved when the fingers have acquired the independence, strength and equality referred to in the preceeding lesson.

In the following exercises we begin with "sec" and "arpeggiando" chords by which initial steps we will arrive at the playing of "effleurez".

Two movements. Whichever of the three ways we use, it is important to remember that we require two distinct movements (1) the tensing of the fingers immediately prior to the plucking of the strings and (2) the instant relaxing of the hand which follows.

Play Exercise (i) and (ii) as "SEC" (i.e.) exactly together.

(1 and 3) - French (2) - Italian.

EXERCISES

Place the first two notes. Prepare the next two while counting the rest and play them exactly together, or "SEC".

(i)

(ii)

Play Exercise (iii) as "arpeggiando" (i.e.) break the chords as an open arpeggio. Make sure to hear all eight notes and place from lowest note upwards. Although the chord is built up in this manner, try to place all four fingers of each hand together as far as possible. Avoid individual "placing" or "straggling".

(iii)

(iv)

(v)

In these exercises we have been experimenting with different keys. Study plan carefully (page 16) and try to learn the Blade changes necessary to change from the "flat" to the "sharp" keys. If you think of C major as a "bridge" over which you must pass from one side to the other, it will be easier. So quite literally, always pass through C major while changing from flats to sharps. Then you add or take away the accidentals as they come and not at random.

SCALE and ARPEGGIO of B flat major and F major.

Moderato = moderate time.

Study No. 3

VINER

Legato = smooth.

The Irish Ho-Hone

Transcribed by
Sheila Larchet-Cuthbert

From "The Fitzwilliam Virginal Book" P.42

THE IRISH HO-HONE - From "The Fitzwilliam Virginal Book" - so-called because it forms an item in the valuable collection of books, music, paintings, etc. left to Cambridge University by Viscount Fitzwilliam in 1816. It used to be known as Queen Elizabeth's Virginal Book but it is now realised that it can never have belonged to her, and that title is abandoned.
cresc. = getting louder

Scarúint Na gCompánach

Arranged by
Sheila Larchet-Cuthbert

Rory Dall Ó Catháin

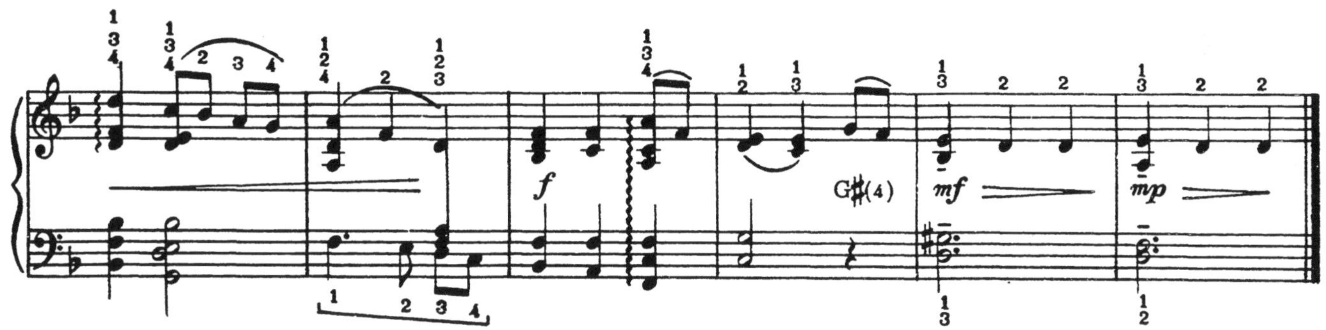

SCARÚINT NA gCOMPÁNACH - Rory Dall Ó Catháin, one of the greatest of the Ulster Harpers who, after the downfall of Hugh O'Neill, resided principally in Scotland. He played before James VI of that Kingdom (James I of England) and died about 1650 at Castle Eglinton, in extreme old age.

«Sons Etouffés» - Gliding - Octaves
Scale and Arpeggio - C MAJOR - 2 Octaves
Studies Nos.4 & 5
Pieces

Miss Hamilton
(Cornelius Lyons)
The Gaelic Farmer
(Treasa Ní Chormaic)

It is now time to consider the question of "Damped Sounds" or "Sons Etouffés" as they are known. This device, one of the most important aspects of Harp playing, requires as much careful attention as the making of sounds, because although the Harp has no sustaining power, it has a considerable amount of vibration from the lower strings. This "overload" of sound must be controlled, otherwise our playing becomes blurred and undefined. The problem does not concern the upper registers of the Harp as vibration at this level is not sufficient to last but we do require the services of the right hand on occasions, to help with the damping of the lower strings.

"Etouffé" is achieved by bringing the palm of the left hand into contact with the vibrating string or strings either rapidly or slowly, according to the required length of the note or notes, thereby causing an immediate "stopping" of the sound. This device is indicated by the sign ⊕ which is usually located below the bass stave.

It is of great importance that "Damping" like "Blading", should be worked into the RHYTHM of the Bar. The Ear suggests the appropriate moments for damping, unless expressly indicated in the music, but the changing of Blades needs to be planned. The ear, of course, will anticipate a coming accidental, but this will not be sufficient to assure accuracy, especially if there are several Blades to be changed.

Etouffés of Single Notes - Open Hand Damping

As a succession of single notes is played, the ball of the thumb drops rapidly onto the string the thumb has just plucked, stopping the sound abruptly. The fingers now take up a quite new position. Instead of turning downwards away from the thumb, they are now pointed upwards and their extremities should lean lightly on the strings to enable the ball of the thumb to damp with rapidity.

And of Two, Three or more Notes

Here the palm of the left hand is used or the palms of both hands, according to the number of strings involved.

Another form, less frequently used but of importance in the playing of STACCATO* with the left hand, is Closed Hand Damping and consists of replacing the same fingers on the vibrating strings immediately they have been played. When playing the lower bass strings it is necessary to use Open Hand, thereby damping the "sounding" notes and moving to the next octave SIMULTANEOUSLY. Damping in upper registers is rarely necessary so the right hand is not concerned in this.

*Italian - separated

OCTAVES

In the playing of octaves, make sure to complete the action of the 4th finger into the palm of the hand and remember to tense and relax the hand as in chord playing.

Right Hand. Closed Hand Damping throughout.

Left Hand. Open Hand Damping for 1st four octaves, change to C. H. and revert to O.H. for last four octaves.

EXERCISES

ETOUFFÉS or DAMPING

'OPEN HAND' Method with thumb playing and damping.

SCALE and ARPEGGIO of C MAJOR (2 OCTAVES)

Practise hands separately and together.

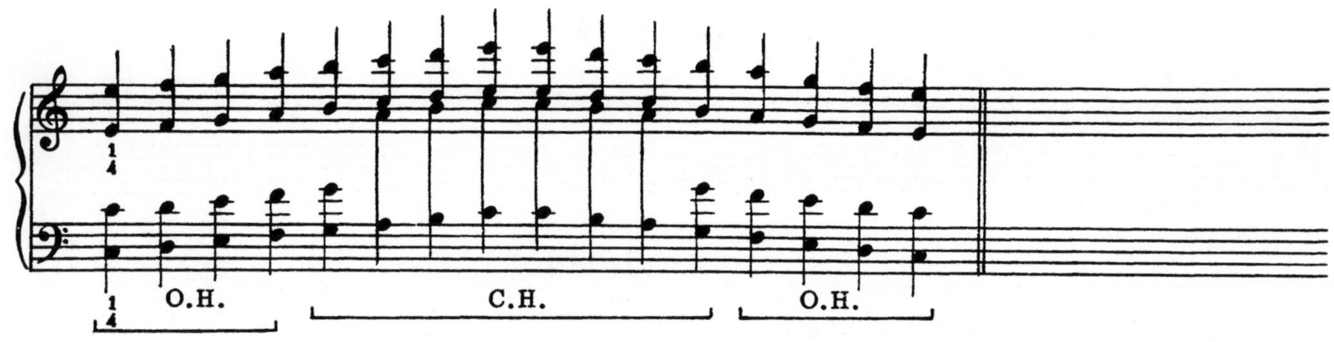

Study No.4

BERTINI

Allegro

f

p

Allegro = Lively, fast.

Study No. 5

Allegro **CZERNY**

f

GLIDING. (Indicated thus ⌒) This manner of fingering was introduced in bar 5 of Study No. 1 (page 27). It can be a useful way of passing smoothly over a group of five consecutive notes when you wish to avoid "pivoting" the hand*. When the notes are ascending, glide with the 4th finger; when descending, with the thumb. But make sure the finger or thumb really glide or slide from one string to the next. If lifted, the effect will not be achieved.

Practise the following examples: left hand one octave lower.

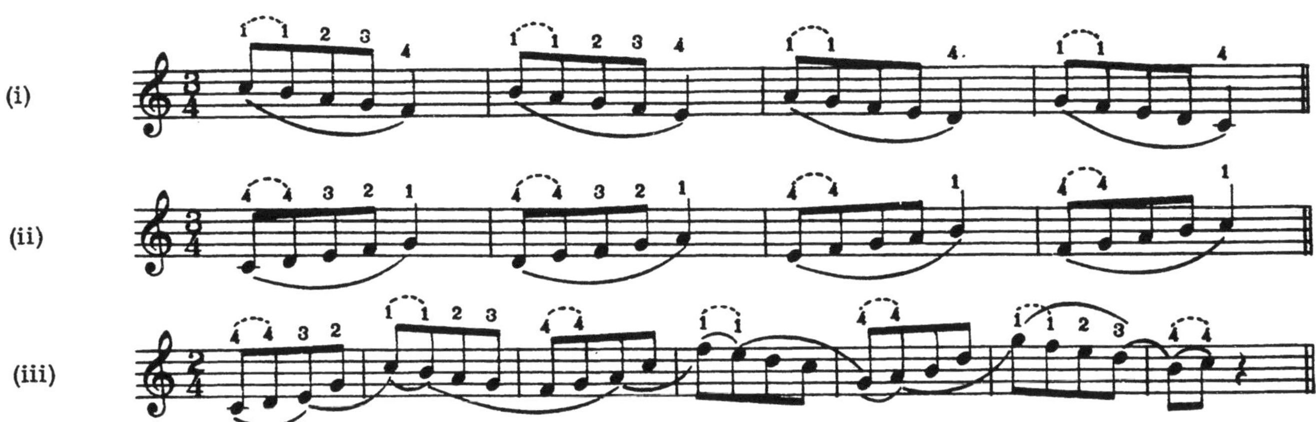

Gradual "placing" will facilitate expansion of hand but the finger which follows the "glide" must always be "prepared".

* "carrying over" the thumb or "under" the 4th, 3rd or 2nd finger.

Miss Hamilton

Arranged by
Sheila Larchet-Cuthbert

Cornelius Lyons in 1706

MISS HAMILTON - was composed about the year 1706 by Cornelius Lyons who was harper to Lord Antrim, the subject probably being one of the Hamiltons of County Tyrone.

*Rallentando = getting slower gradually.

The Gaelic Farmer

Taken down from Treasa Ní Chormaic
by Mercedes McGrath

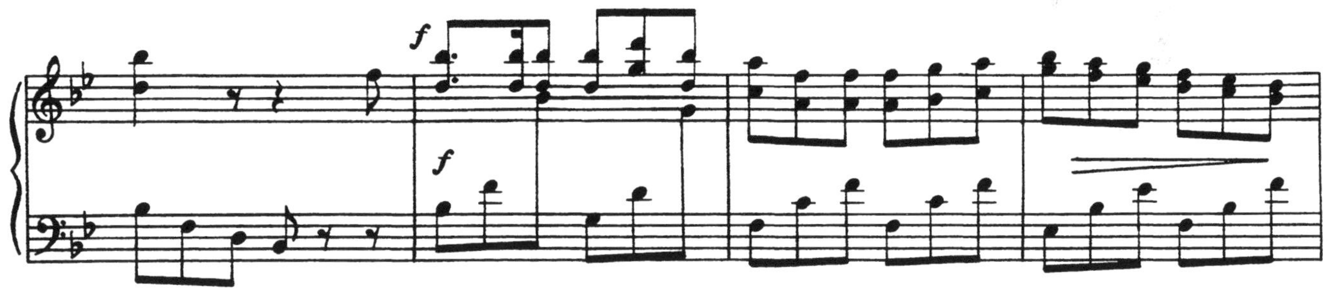

LESSON V

Harmonics
Scales and Arpeggios - G MAJOR and D MAJOR
Studies Nos. 6 & 7
Pieces

William O'Flinn
(Carolan)
Lament and Hornpipe (Bunting Collection)
(Treasa Ní Chormaic)
I will leave this country
David Foy
} (Petrie Collection)
(Mercedes McGrath)

HARMONICS (Indicated thus: o) The production of Harmonic sounds is one of the most charming effects of Harp playing but it is a very delicate device requiring care and "occasion".

Harmonics are produced in the right hand by placing the two upper joints of the first finger (pointing downwards, as usual) against the middle of the string and then using the thumb to pluck the string; in the left hand by placing the ball of the thumb against the middle of the string and using the upper part of the thumb to pluck. There are two points to remember: (i) the Harmonic will only "speak" at one particular point of the string, near the middle, and (ii) a Harmonic must never be forced. Such a movement of the finger or thumb will produce only a dull, percussive sound. Coax the sound gently from the string and immediately draw the hand slightly back to release the resonance.

The Harmonic, of course, sounds one octave higher than the written note.

Owing to the lack of vibration in the upper octaves of the Irish Harp, the end of the safe harmonic range is approximately 2nd octave G. Finally, harmonics speak more clearly when the string is in its most relaxed position; i.e. when blades are not being used.

Try the following examples, very slowly at first. The key of E flat will make it easier.

Note: Wire strings will not give satisfactory results, so we do not usually write harmonics for these.

DOUBLE or TRIPLE HARMONICS. When two or more notes are to be played, in the 3rd or 4th octave, the lower part of the left hand, near the wrist, is placed against the strings while the thumb and first finger are used to pluck the required notes. In the 2nd octave double harmonics are best divided between the left thumb and right first finger.

QUADRUPLE HARMONICS are divided between the hands, the right playing the top note.

HARMONICS

(i)
R.H.

(ii)
L.H.

(iii)
R.H.
L.H.

SCALE and ARPEGGIO - G Major

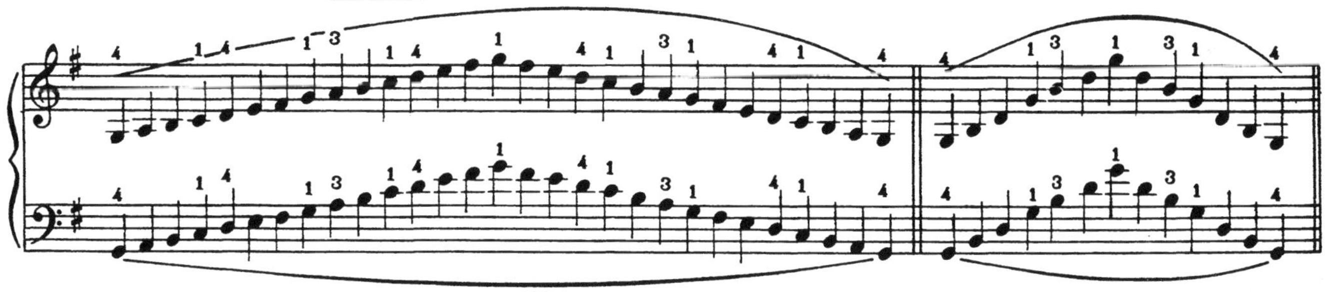

D Major

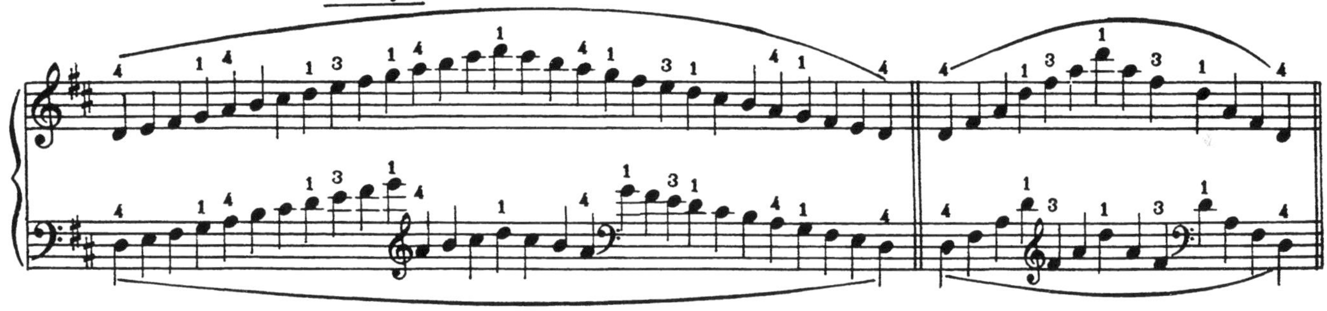

OCTAVES with Extension of 'Gliding'. Also involving Chords - Double and Triple Glides with Descending Thumb Glides.

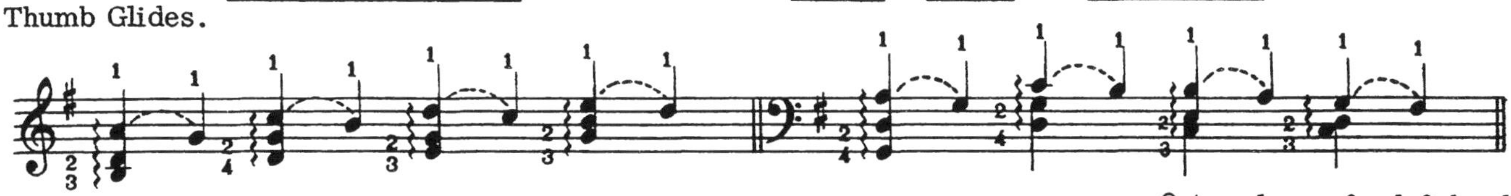

Octave lower for left hand

(i)

(ii)

(iii)

Study No. 6

Study No. 7

CZERNY

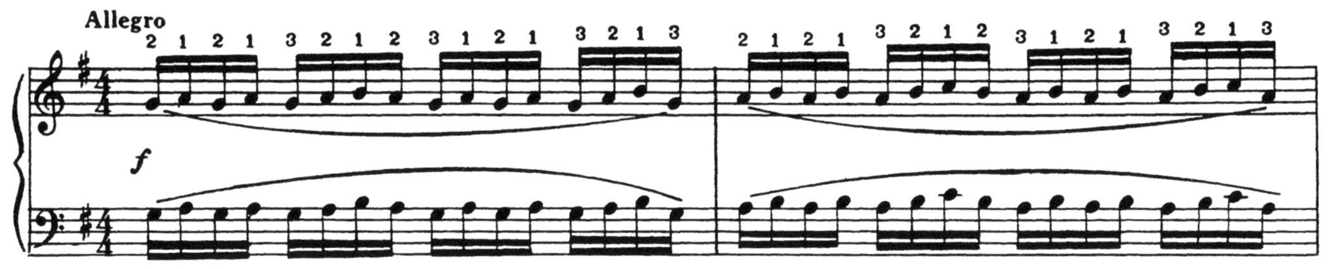

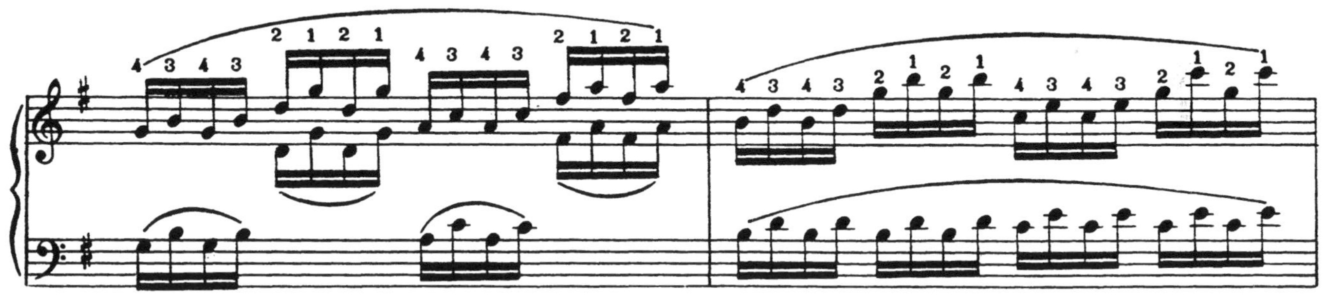

William O'Flinn

Arranged by
Sheila Larchet-Cuthbert

CAROLAN

WILLIAM O'FLINN - Turlough O'Carolan (1670-1738) was the last of the Irish Harper-composers and the only one whose pieces have survived in any number; about two hundred are extant. Carolan was blinded by smallpox in early youth and adopted music as a career. His genius for making melody manifested itself almost at once, and for nearly fifty years he travelled the Irish countryside, staying at the great houses and entertaining the company with his playing and singing. The great majority of his pieces were composed in honour of his patrons and in most cases he devised verses to fit the music. He was also a familiar figure in Dublin where he must have heard the music of Corelli, Vivaldi and Geminiani. He was much charmed by this music, then fashionable, and imitated the music of Corelli in its form and melodic idiom in certain of his pieces. This composition is one such example.

Vivace = Quick, lively.

Lament and Hornpipe

Arranged by
Mercedes Bolger

Bunting Collection
2. Treasa Ní Chormaic

Doloroso = Sorrowfully

a piacere = at pleasure   bis = twice

Tempo I = Resume the original speed.

I Will Leave This Country And Go Along With You

(To Wander Under The Arches Of The Blossomed Woods)

Arranged by
Mercedes McGrath

Petrie Collection

Andante = At a moderate pace

mf
mf
B♮(3)
rit.
a tempo
cresc.
B♮(2)
f
f
dim.
sim.
dim. e rall.
pp

David Foy

Arranged by
Mercedes McGrath

Petrie Collection

Ad lib (libitum) = At pleasure

Andantino = Alternatively faster or slower than Andante.

A♮(2) ♭
mf
f
p
1
2
7
6
3
1
3
pp
2
1

LESSON VI

Recapitulation
Scales and Arpeggios ~ A MAJOR and E MAJOR
Studies Nos. 8, 9 and 10
Pieces

Suite of Four Pieces for Three Harps (Anne Crowley)
Maurice O'Connor (Carolan)
For The Children (Edgar M. Deale)-
(Two Pieces with Harp Accompaniment)

At this halfway stage, it is useful to recapitulate the various points of basic technique introduced in the preceding chapters and to realise that they are only the means by which we build up a technique over the years. There is no short-cut to this essential process and the fingers are ever "in training". Such is our physical make-up that having built up a technique, we must work to keep it!

Scale practice is of the greatest value and should never be neglected, however short the practice-time.

SCALE and ARPEGGIO of A MAJOR (2 octaves)

SCALE and ARPEGGIO of E MAJOR (2 octaves)

Octaves as in Lesson V but in new keys of A and E major.

Glissando - The rapid playing of a scale or series of notes by drawing the thumb downwards and the fore-finger upwards on the strings, can be one of the most exciting effects in harp playing. A glissando (from the French word "glisser" to slide) is indicated thus:

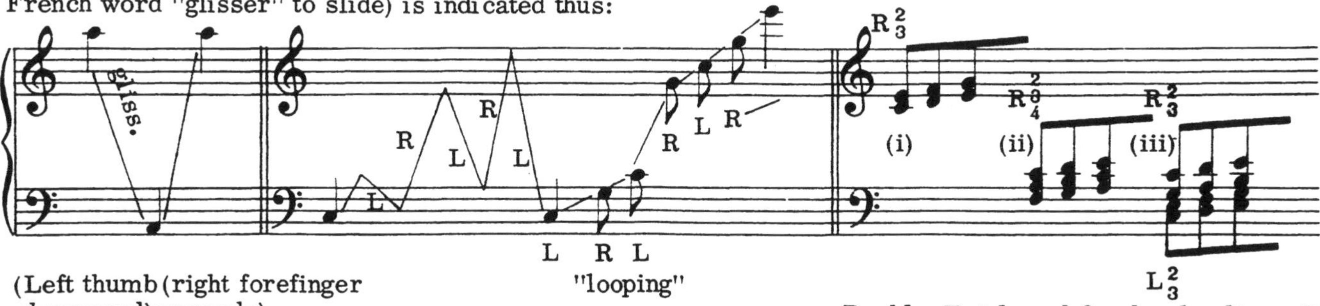

L R L
"looping"

L 2/3

(Left thumb (right forefinger downward) upwards)
They can be doubled, of course and played at any speed.

Double, Triple and Quadruple glissandi are also possible. ((i) and (ii) can also be divided between the two hands.)

Study No. 8

CZERNY

Study No. 9

SCHUMANN

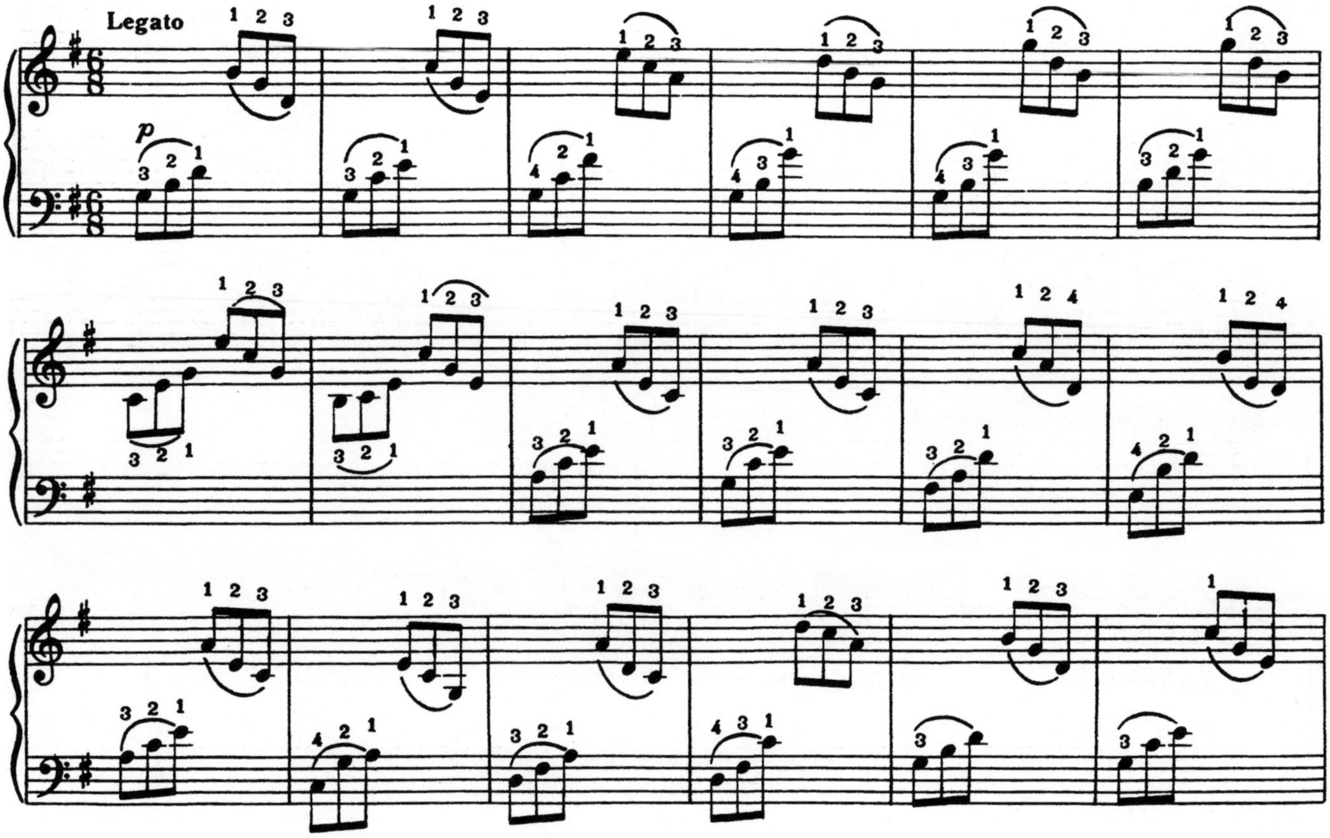

Legato

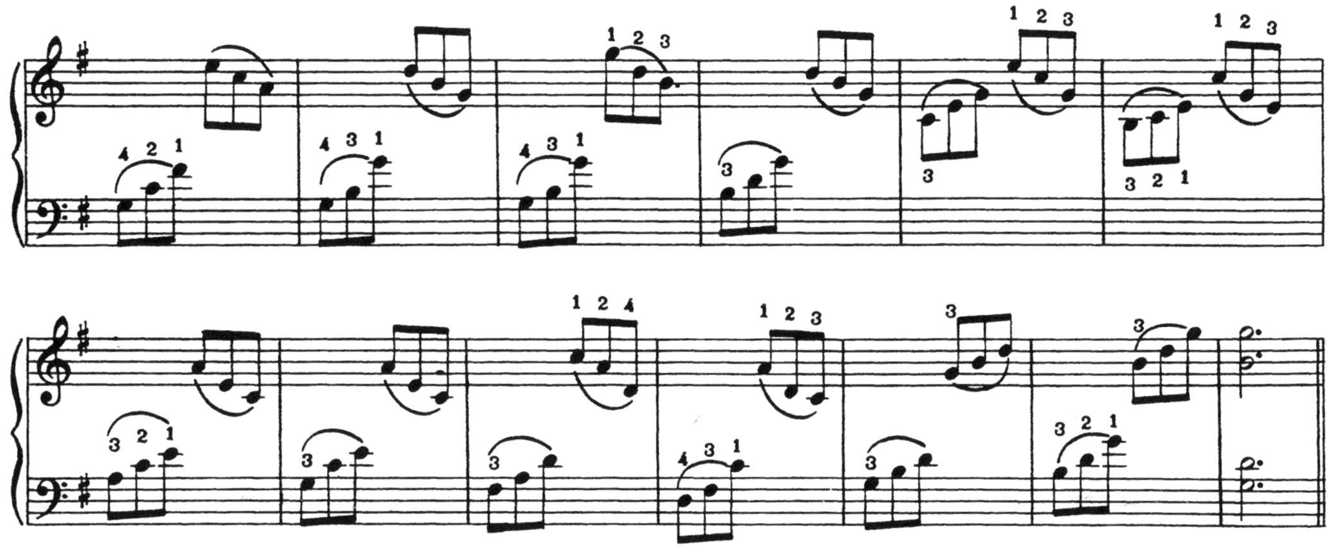

Study No. 10

CHALLONER

Moderato

Hornpipe

1st Harp Solo

Anne Crowley

The composer desires that each member of the Trio will play a Solo Part.
HORNPIPE - A lively dance.

Hornpipe

f
mf
p
mf solo
mf
mf solo

f
solo
mf
solo
f
solo
f
8
ff
ff
ff
ff
ff
ff

SOLO

Single Jig

SINGLE JIG - A lively dance.

Single Jig

solo
L.H.

gliss

Suantraí

SOLO

Sostenuto e espressivo = sustained and expressive

Suantraí = A Cradle Song

Suantraí

TRIO
Harp I
dolce e legato
Harp II
Harp III
L.H.
R.H.
cresc.
cresc.
cresc.

dim.
dim.
dim.
mf
mf
mf

dim. e rall.
a tempo
dim. e rall.
a tempo
dim. e rall.
a tempo
dim.
ppp
dim.
ppp
dim.
ppp

Reel

REEL - A lively dance.

rall.
pp
me o p
rall.
pp
meno p
pp
meno p
mf
mf
mf

solo
rall.
ppp
rall.
ppp
ppp
rall.
ppp
p
p
ff
mf

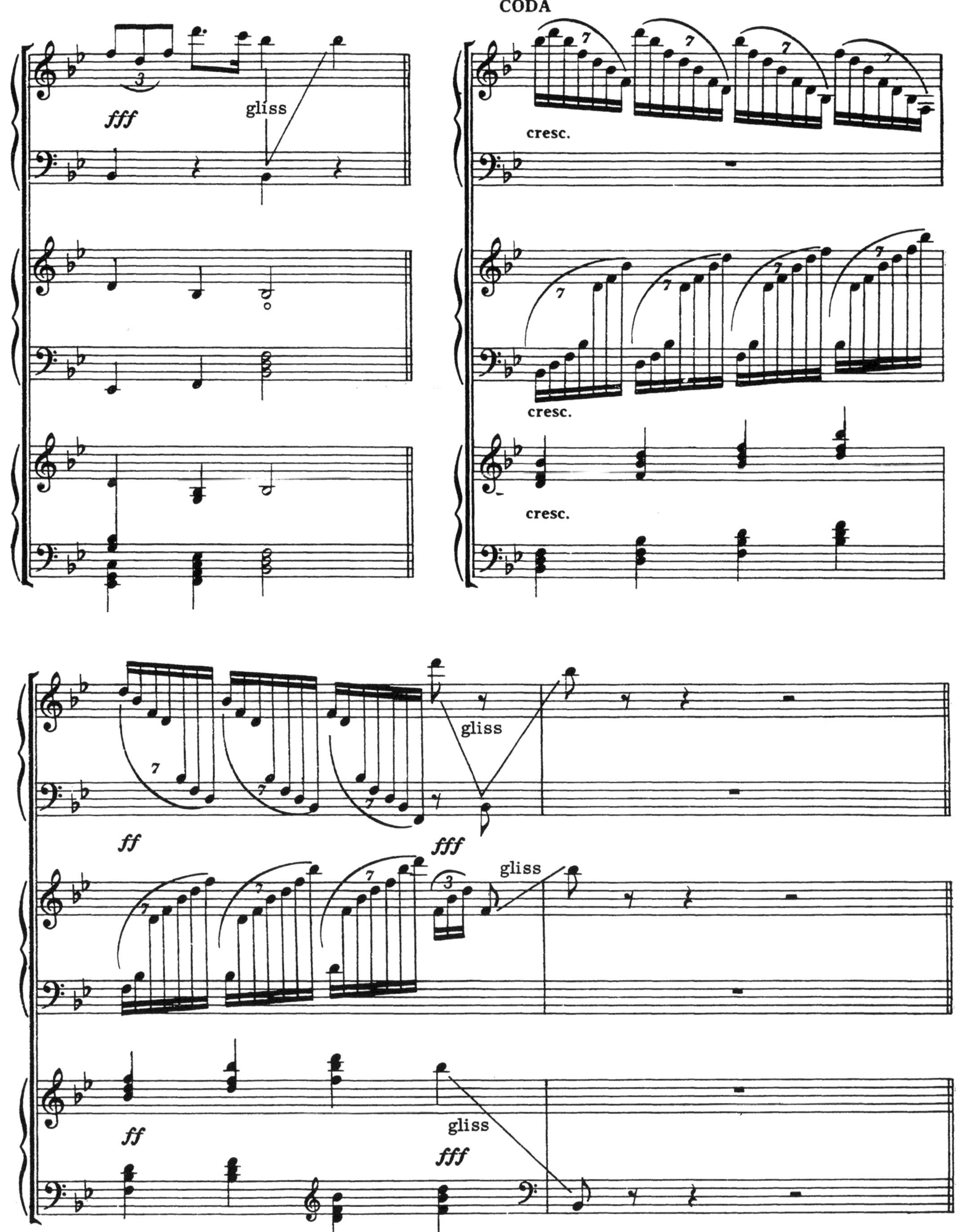

CODA
fff
gliss
cresc.
cresc.
cresc.
ff
fff
gliss
gliss
ff
gliss
fff

Maurice O'Connor

Arranged by
Sheila Larchet-Cuthbert

CAROLAN

MAURICE O'CONNOR - was head, in Carolan's day, of the O'Connors of Offaly. He went to England to seek his fortune and became a member of the Inner Temple and one of the great leaders of the English Bar.

Grazioso = Gracefully *mf* (mezzo forte) = moderately loud.

For The Children

No. 1 Song Without Words

EDGAR M. DEALE

20
25
30
35

40
45
pp
dim.
p
50
55
mp/mf
cresc.
f

60
65
70
dim. e rall.
dim. e rall.

For The Children

No. 2 SET DANCE

EDGAR M. DEALE

8
15
loco
20
8
8

25
loco
30
35

8
40
loco
45

Exercises

Minor Scales (Relative - Harmonic)
C Minor - G Minor - D Minor
Scales, 2 octaves, Arpeggios and
Inversions, Sixths and Tenths,
Octaves

Studies Nos. 11, 12 & 13

Pieces

An Cóitín Dearg
(Aloys Fleischmann)
John Kelly
(Carolan)

Songs

An Spailpín Fánach
(arr. Carrie Townshend)
Dilín Ó Deamhas
(arr. Máirín Ní Shé)

It may have come as a surprise to many that songs have not been introduced until now, the beginning of the second part of this Tutor. The reason is obvious. You cannot play for yourself until you can play and self-accompaniment on the Harp is not nearly as simple as it appears. In this complex and highly skilled art, the player is obliged to divide attention equally between the two parts and must be both soloist and sympathetic accompanist all at once. Much concentrated practice is required before this artistic result can be achieved, but it is worth the effort!

MINOR SCALES - HARMONIC FORM (For Chart see page 16)

C MINOR - Relative Minor of E FLAT MAJOR.

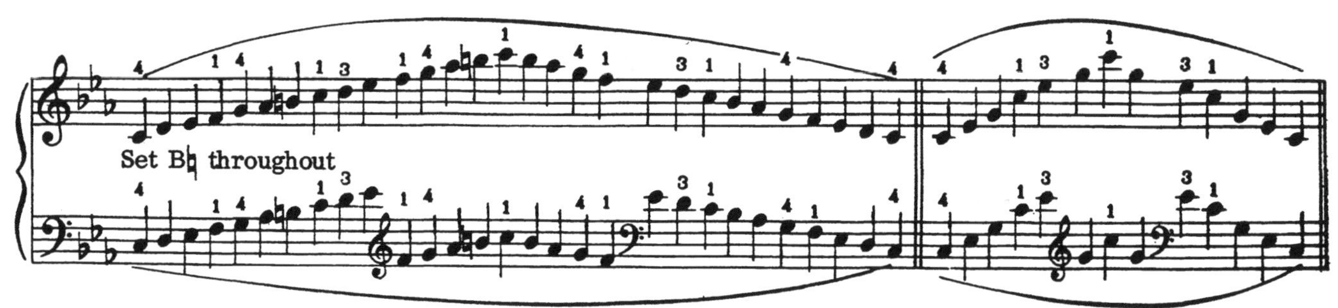

C MINOR (Continued)

IN SIXTHS

IN TENTHS

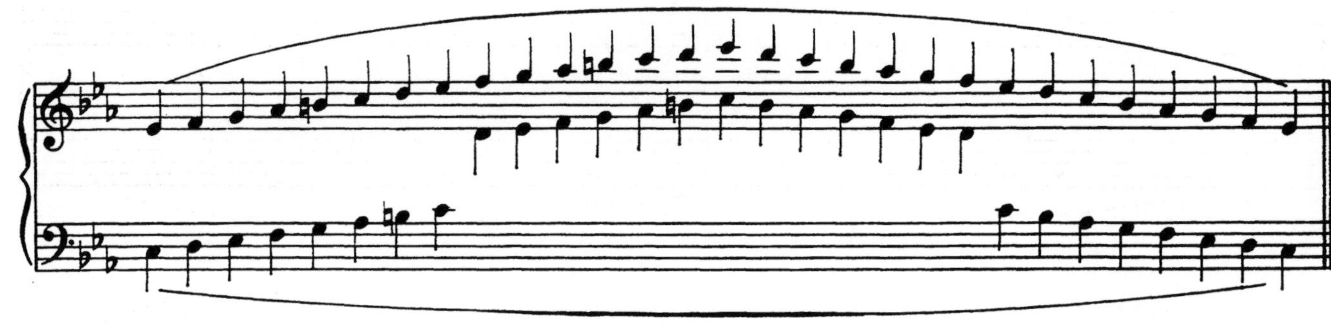

G MINOR - Relative Minor of B FLAT MAJOR

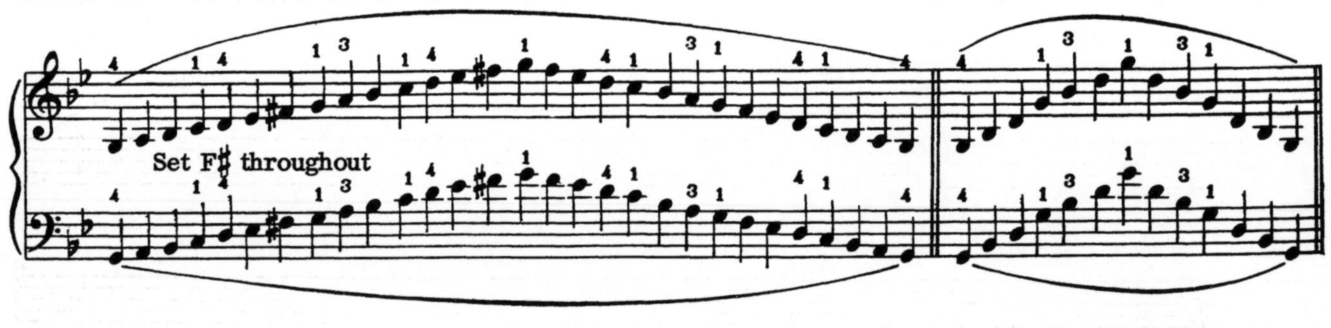

SIXTHS

TENTHS

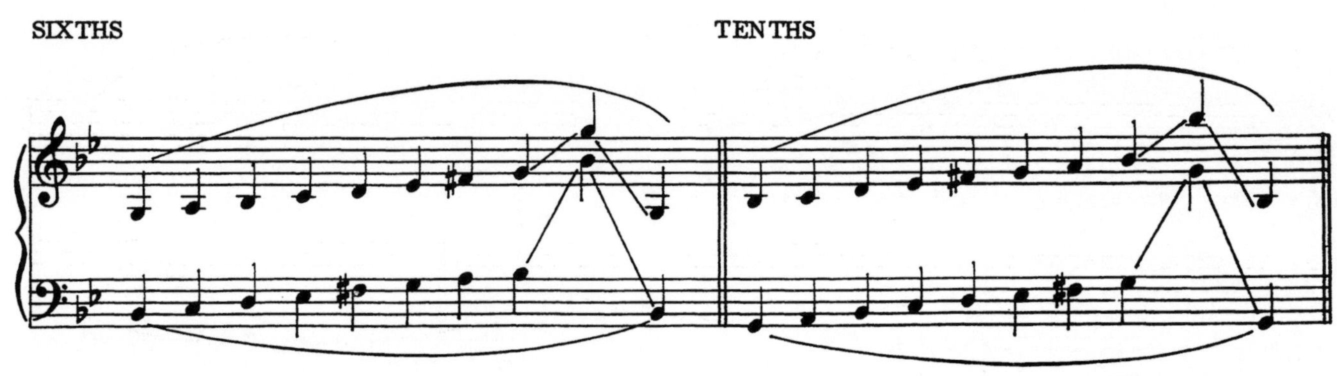

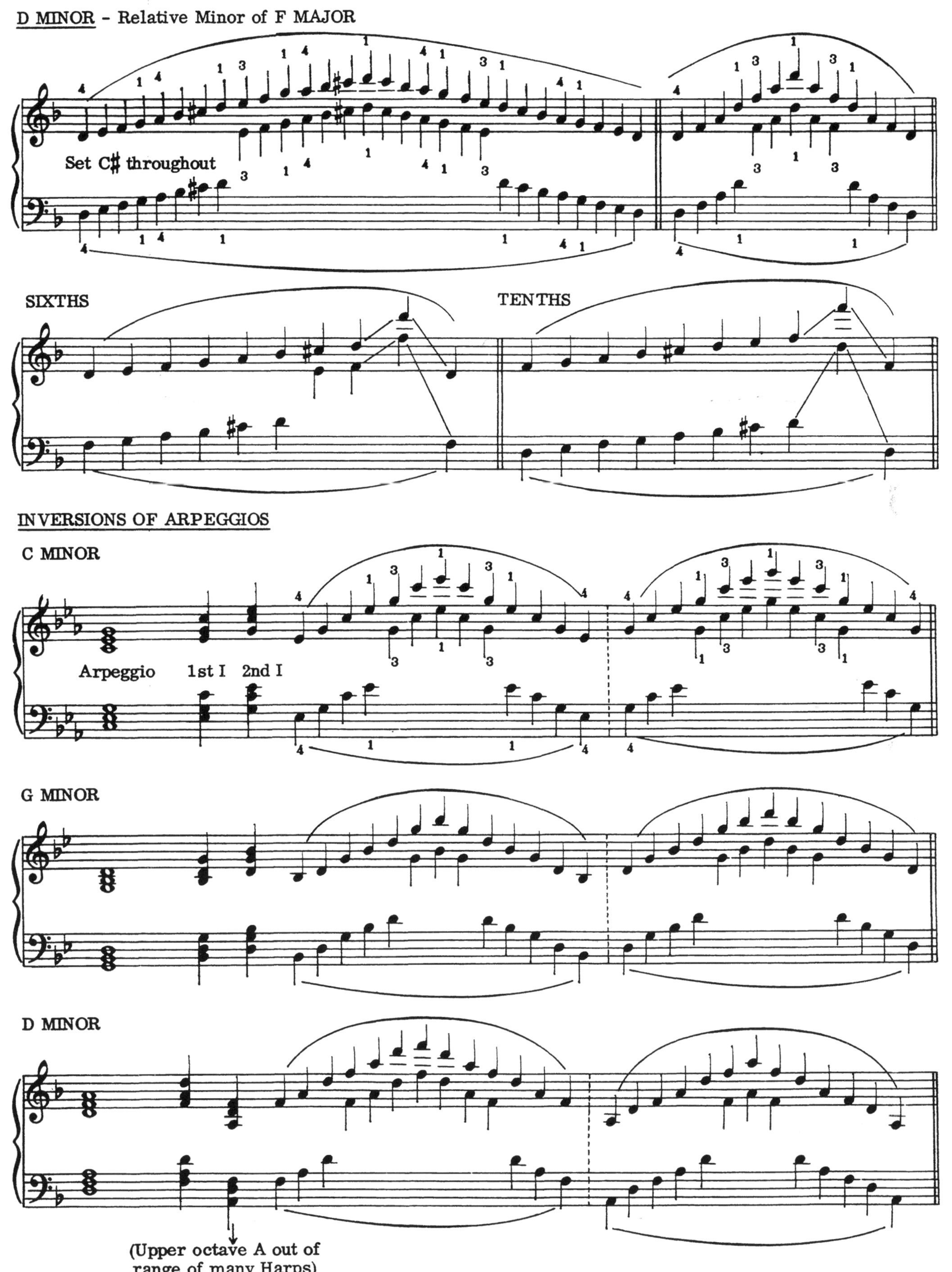
D MINOR - Relative Minor of F MAJOR
Set C♯ throughout
SIXTHS
TENTHS
INVERSIONS OF ARPEGGIOS
C MINOR
Arpeggio
1st I
2nd I
G MINOR
D MINOR
(Upper octave A out of range of many Harps)

Study No.11
CHALLONER
Andantino
p
Study No. 12
CHALLONER
Moderato

Study No. 13

VINER

Con moto = With movement

An Cóitín Dearg

ALOYS FLEISCHMANN

Allegretto Scherzando = Rather lively and playfully

L'istesso tempo = the same speed

molto = much

ff
A♭(2)
f
6
6
p
pp
IV Tempo primo
A♮(2)
mp
p
pp
mp
pp
p
pp
ppp

Arranged by
Sheila Larchet-Cuthbert

John Kelly

Carolan

ten. (tenuto) = held

JOHN KELLY - The subject of this graceful air is not certain, but it may have been either of two people; Colonel John Kelly of Skreen, Co. Roscommon or John Kelly of Castle Kelly or Aghrane Castle, Cloonlyon.

An Spailpín Fánach

Arranged by
CARRIE TOWNSHEND

An Spailpín Fánach

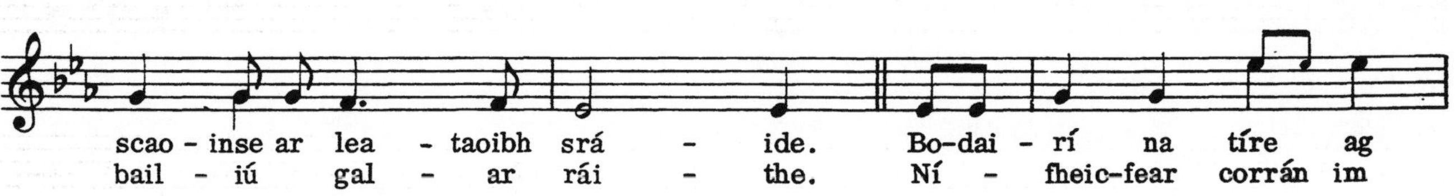

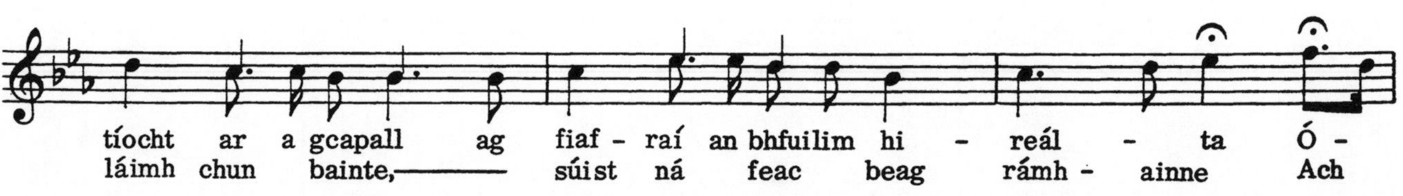

Dilín Ó Deamhas

(TRADITIONAL)

MÁIRÍN NÍ SHÉ
a chóirigh

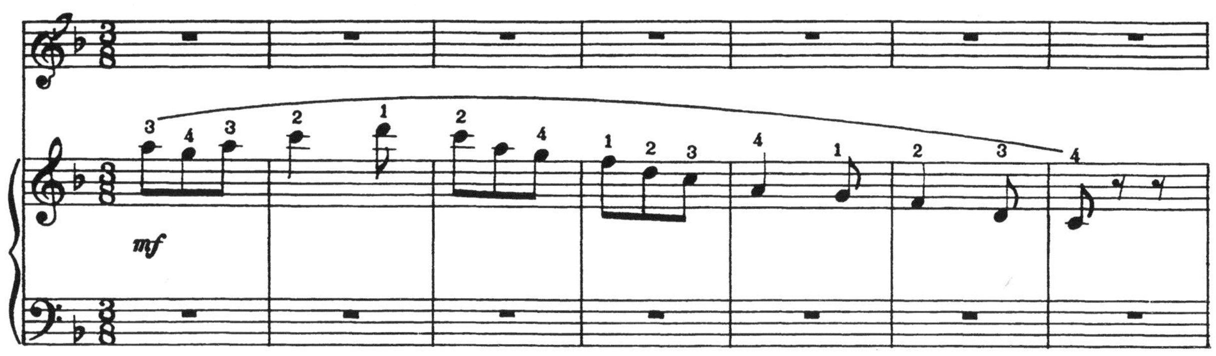

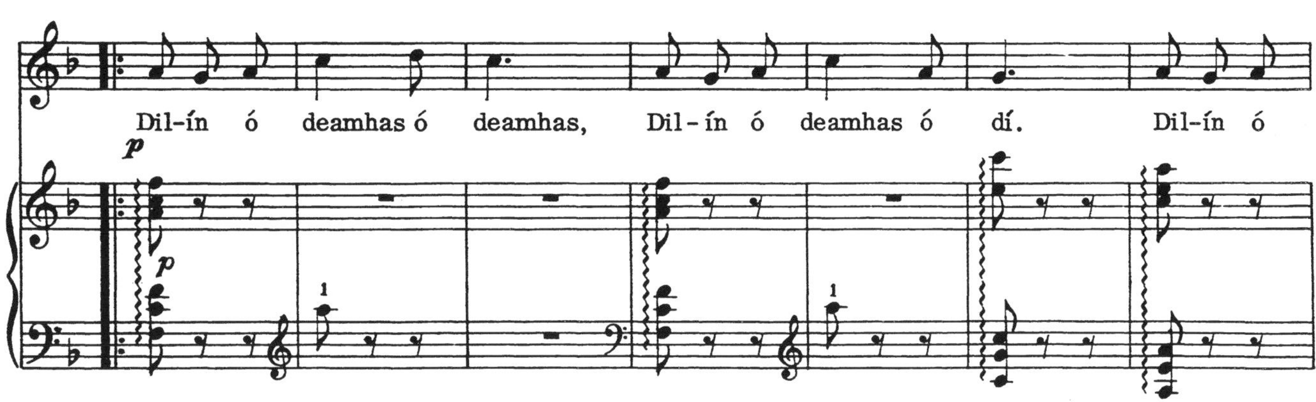

mf
Cuirfead mo rún chun suain, Cuirfead mo rún 'na luí Cuirfead mo
mf
rún chun suain go ciúin le Di-lín ó deamhas ó dí.
rit.
rit.
pp a tempo
Dil-ín ó deamhas ó deamhas, Dil-ín ó deamhas ó dí. Dil-ín ó
a tempo
pp
deamhas ó deamhas ó deamhas ó Dil-ín ó deamhas ó dí.
pp

Exercises

Scales - 2 Octaves
Arpeggios and Inversions
Sixths and Tenths
Continuing MINORS
A minor - E minor

Studies Nos. 14, 15 & 16

Pieces

Allegro Giocoso
(John Kinsella)
Farewell to Music
(Carolan)

Songs

Máire Ní Eidhin
(Arr. Róisín Ní Shé)
Anonn 's Anall
(Arr. Gráinne Yeats)

A MINOR - Relative minor of C MAJOR.

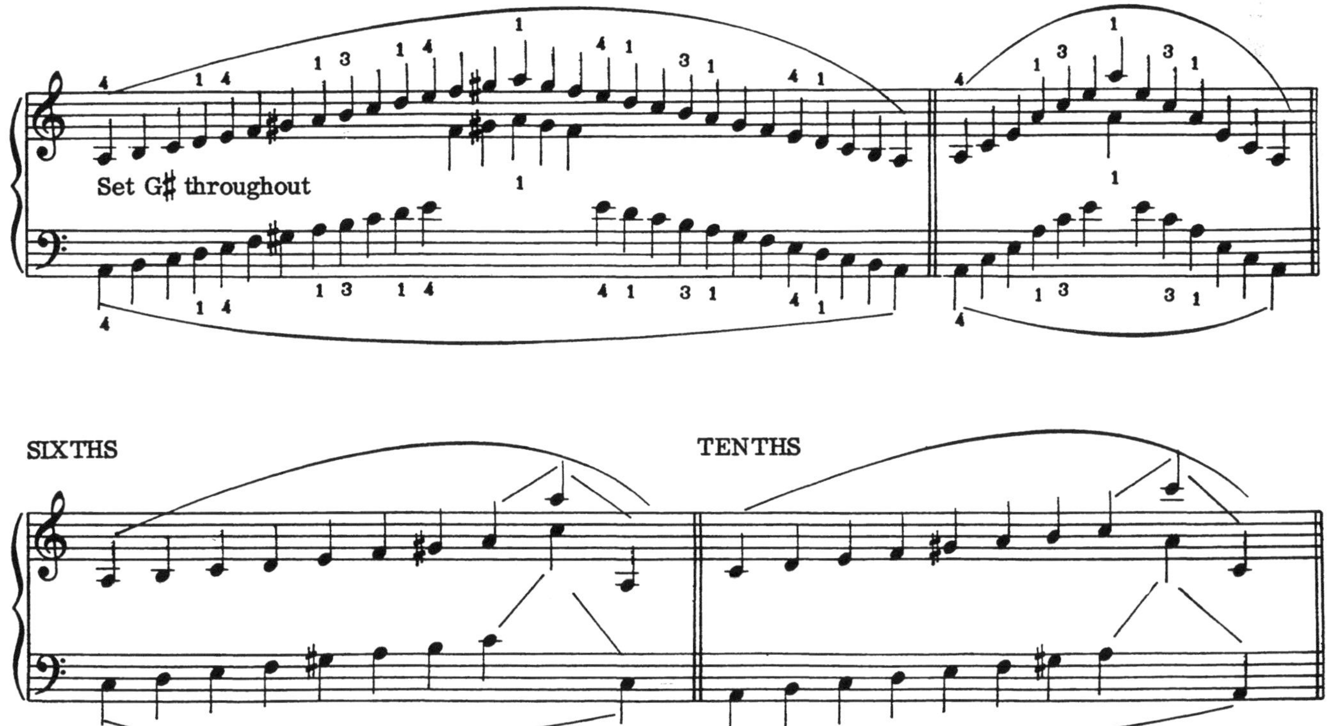

E MINOR - Relative minor of G MAJOR.

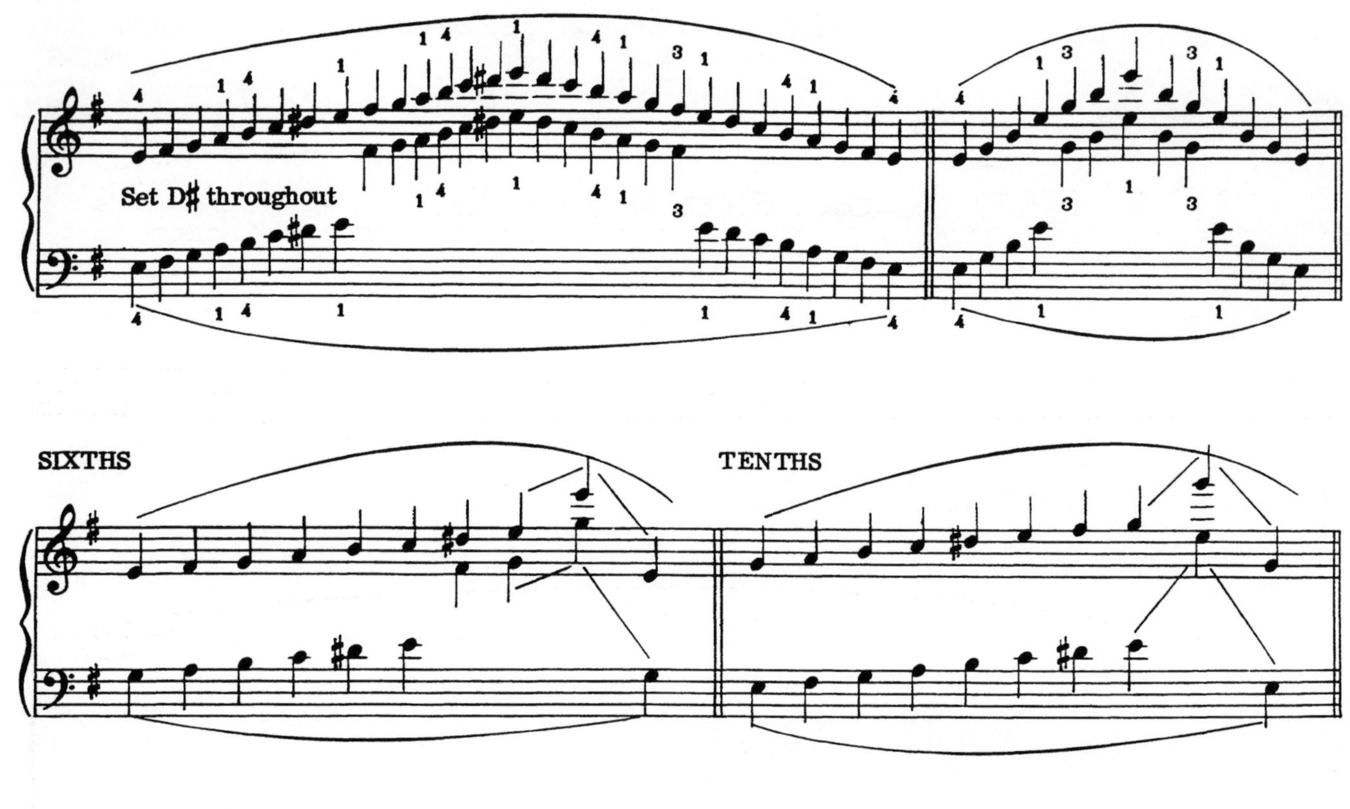

INVERSIONS OF ARPEGGIOS

Study No. 14

VINER

Study No. 15

VINER

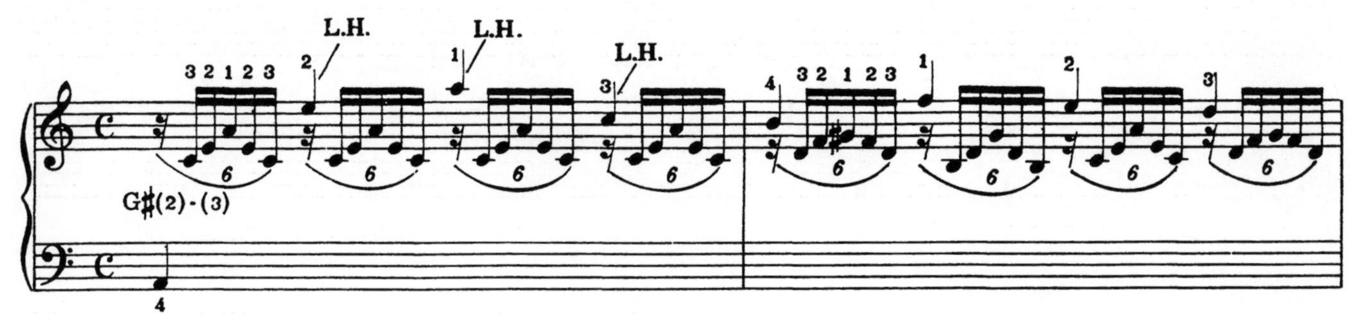

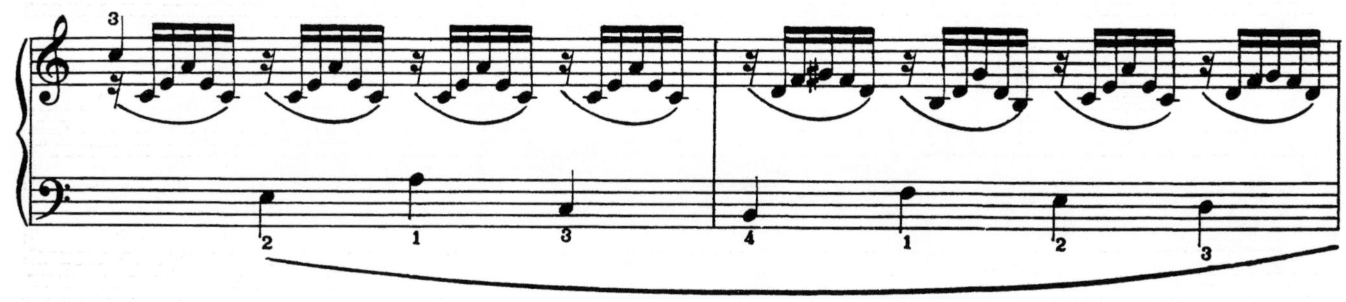

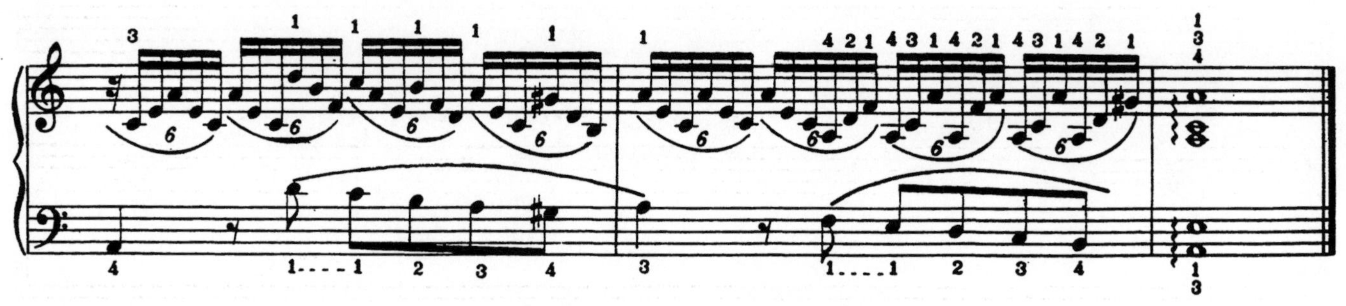

Study No. 16

Moderato **MEYER**

Allegro Giocoso

JOHN KINSELLA

Giocoso = Gay, merry
Subito = suddenly
Près de la table (PDLT) = near the soundboard
Ben marcato = well marked

Tranquillo = Calm
Accel. = Gradually faster

Tempo primo (𝅗𝅥=132)
giocoso
f
cresc.
ff
f
subito p
subito mp
mf
f
mf cresc.
ff

Carolan's Farewell To Music

Arranged by
Sheila Larchet-Cuthbert

Adagio = Slow

FAREWELL TO MUSIC - This was Carolan's last piece. He came home to Alderford to die and was received by his aged patroness Mrs. MacDermott Roe. He called for his harp, played this tune, and was then led upstairs to what was to be his death-bed.

Máire Ní Eidhin

RÓISÍN NÍ SHÉ
a chóirigh

Máire Ní Eidhin

ANTÓIN Ó REACHTABHRA

Ar mo dhul chuig an Aifreann le toil na nGrásta, Bhí'n lá 'cur báistí is
Sí Máire Ní Eidhin an stáidbhean bhéasach Ba dheise méin agus

d'ardaigh gaoth, Casadh an ainnir liom le taob Chill Tártain Is thit- mé láithreach i
b'áille gnaoi, Dhá— chéad cléireach 's a gcur le chéile Agus trian a tréithre ní

ngrá le mnaoi. Do labhair mé léi go múin - te mánla, 'S de réir a cáillíocht' do
fhéad-fadh scríobh; Bhuail sí Déirdre le breáthacht 's Véineas, Is dá n-abrainn Hel - en ler

fhreagair sí, 'Sé dúirt sí - "Raft'rí, tá m'intinn sásta, 'Gus gluais go lá liom go Baile Uí Laí.
scriosadh an Traoi- Ach scoth ban Éireann as ucht an mhéid sin An pósae— gléigeal 'tá i mBaile Uí Laí.

Shiúil mé Sasana 's an Fhrainc le chéile
An Spáinn, an Ghréig 's ar ais arís
Ó bhruach loch Gréine go Béal na Céibhe
'S ní fhaca mé féirín ar bith mar í.
Dá mbeinnse pósta le bláth na hóige
Trí Loch an Toraic do leanfainn í,
Cuanta 's cóstaí do shiúlfainn 's bóithre
I ndiaidh an tseoidbhean 'tá i mBaile Uí Laí

Anonn's Anall

Focail:
COLM Ó LOCHLAINN

Chóirigh:
GRÁINNE YEATS

pp
p
'Nonn 's a-nall 'nonn 's a-nall. Ó thuaidh tá éan-laith 'n tsléibh a' filleadh, Foluain a-nonn 's a-
pp
p
mp
-nall. 'S gearr, a stór, go n-éirigh an ghealach A' scal-ladh seod thar far-raige 's sliabh
mp poco cresc.
decresc.
mp
p
Suaimhneas ar domhan, a ro-gha 's a mhúirnín 'Luascadh 'nonn 's anall.
p
mp
mp
p
mp
A chúil-ín óir, a stór mo chroí-se, 'Nonn 's a-nall, 'nonn 's a-nall, Go
mp
simile
p

perpendosi = dying away

Anonn's Anall

Focail:
COLM Ó LOCHLAINN

Exercises

Scales: all keys, Contrary Motion
Arpeggios and Inversions, Contrary Motion

Studies Nos. 17, 18 & 19

Pieces

John O'Connor
(Carolan)
Interlude
(T. C. Kelly)

Songs

An Fhallaingín Mhuimhneach
(Arr. Ruth Mervyn)
Grá Mo Chroí Thú Éire
(Arr. Nancy Calthorpe)
Do Chuala Scéal
(Cian Ó hÉigeartaigh)

CONTRARY MOTION - in ONE Octave

Make sure to play Left Thumb and Right Fourth Finger exactly together on the starting note. Also, pay particular attention to "replacement" of fingers at the "return".

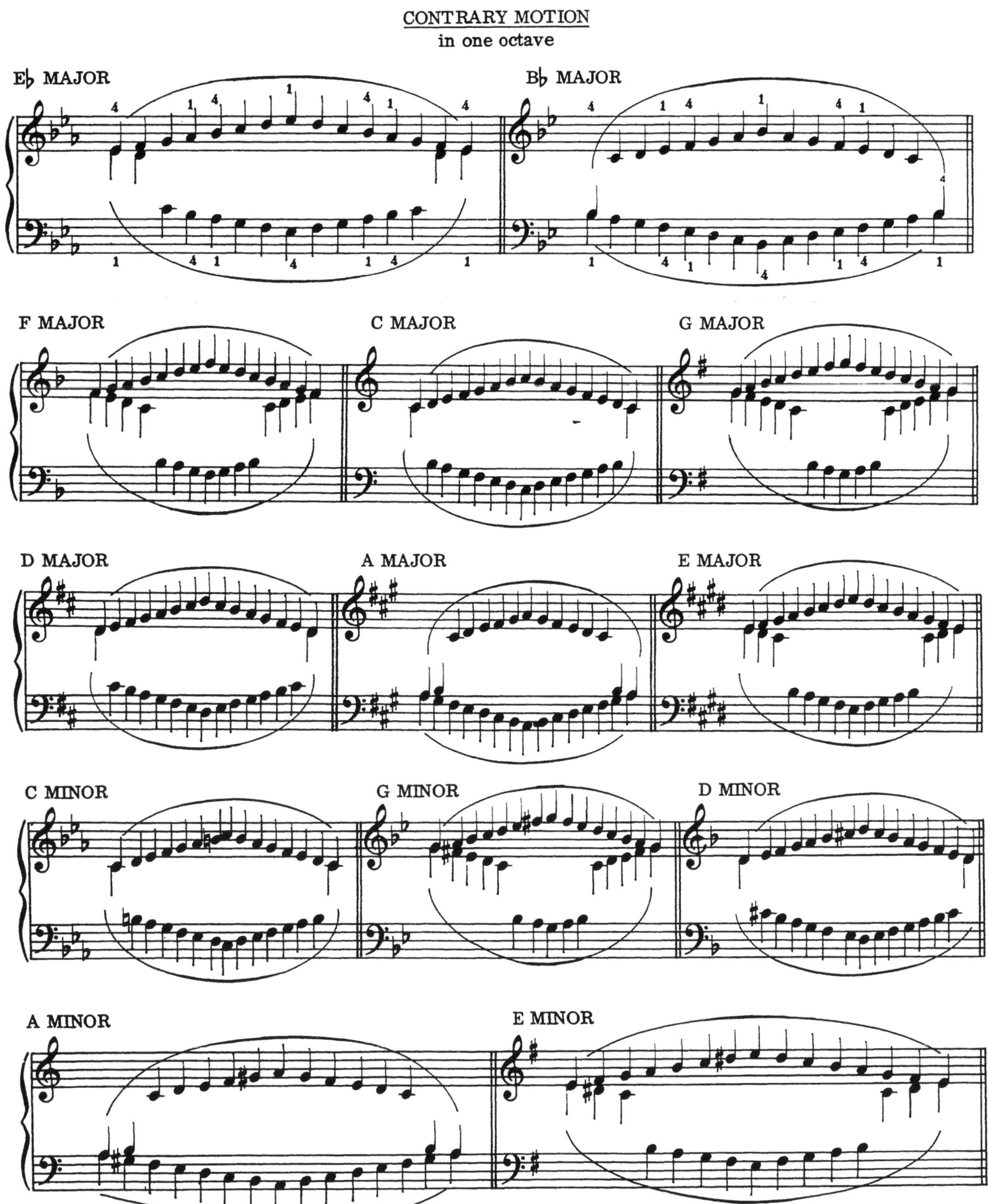

ARPEGGIOS and INVERSIONS OF ARPEGGIOS CONTRARY MOTION

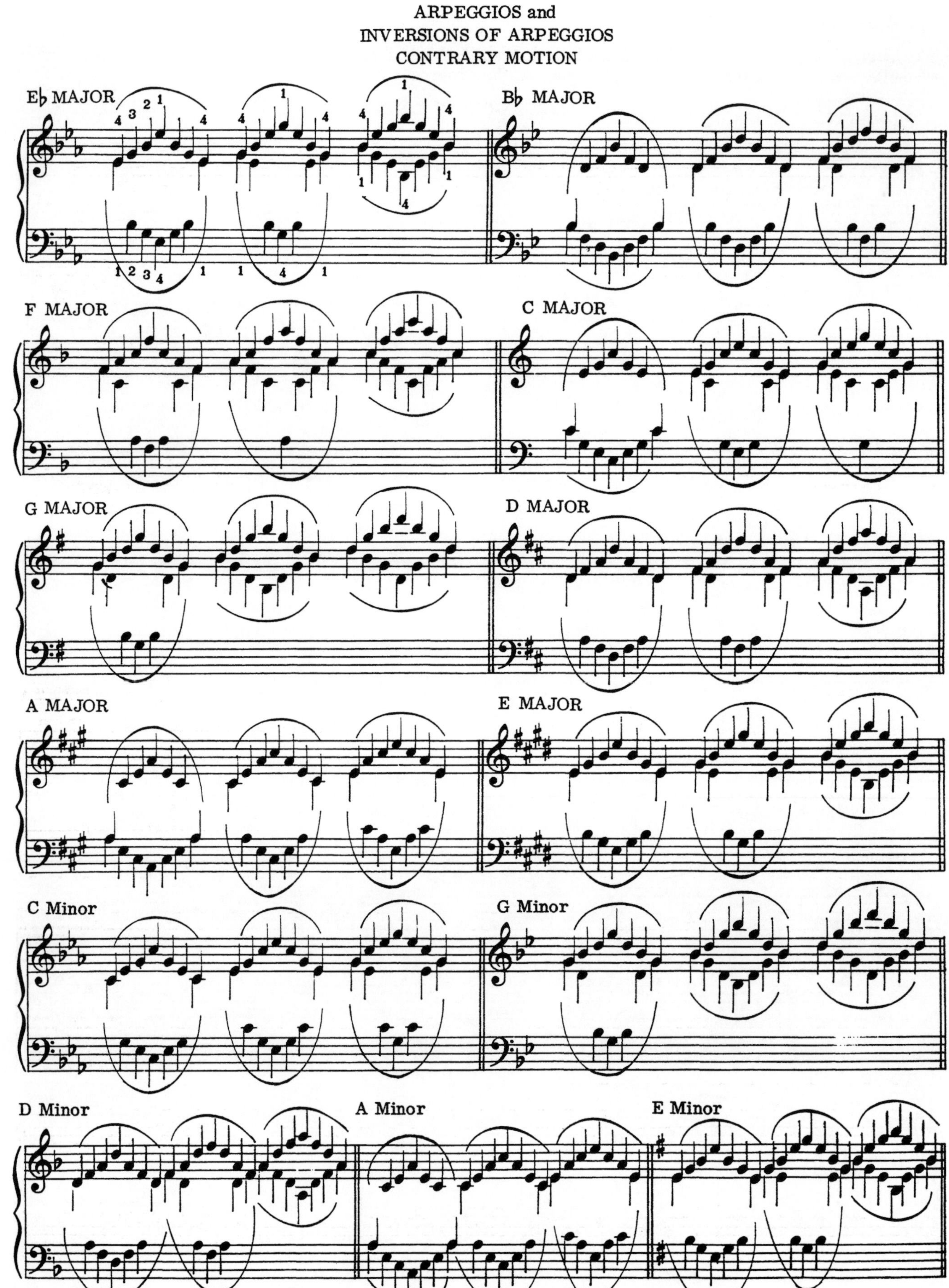

Study No. 17

CARDON FILS

Study No. 18

Andantino

BOCHSA

Study No. 19

CZERNY

Arranged by
Sheila Larchet-Cuthbert

John O'Connor

CAROLAN

"JOHN O'CONNOR" - This is one of the best known of Carolan's livelier melodies. Counsellor John O'Connor was one of the O'Connors of Offaly.

Interlude

T. C. KELLY

Meno = Less Pocissimo = As small as possible 8va (Ottava) = An octave higher

Rubato = (literally) Robbed, stolen, taking a portion of the duration from one note or group of notes and adding it to another, so that although the detail varies, the length of the phrase is normal.

poco = a little loco = place, i.e. at normal pitch

f
f
(L.H.)
cresc.
poco a poco
rall. molto
accel.
(L.H.)
a tempo
accel.
(L.H.)
poco rall.
f
gliss.
8

Dr. A Patterson

An Fhallaingín Mhuimhneach

a chóirigh
RUTH MERVYN

sempre tempo giusto = always in strict time

Deciso = decisively

Attacca = Go on at once   Con fuoco = with fire

Grá Mo Chroí Thú, Éire

Focail:
T.A. Ó Rathaille
Arranged
Nancy Calthorpe

-nois, mo léan, Faoi chois ag namhaid gan tru - a, Ach
LH RH
over
LH RH
táirse - ag siúl chun saoir - se Gair - id uait an
LH over
bua. Ar maid - in lae na
rall.
LH LH
saoir - se Chí - fear á - thas ar gach croí Beidh brat na tíre in
LH RH LH
over
LH
LH
LH

air - de 'sé glas is bán is buí; Faoi
LH RH LH
sliabh is gleann Beidh ceol is greann 'S an rin - - ce fa - da
Tempo giusto
leo. Grá mo chroí thú, Éir - e, 'Gus
rall.
a tempo
slán a bhéir go deo.
rall. - - - -

Do Chuala Scéal

Focail:
le Piaras Feirtéir

CIAN Ó hÉIGEARTAIGH

i lea-ba na leo-mhan, Go seas-cair sámh, go sódh-úil seo-mrach,
Brío-mhar, bi-a-mhar, briathrach, bór-dmhar, Coimhthíoch, caint-
-each, sain-teach, sró - nach.
3. Furioso
f
Gríosú cnead laghdú ar neart, síó-
3
5

rú ar cheas — bró - nach, Fío - rú ár bhfear do gheimhliú i nglas, —
foil - siú a n-acht — óir - - nne, Críoch-nú ár bhflaith do dhío-rú a-mach ar
dhroim tonn — thar bóch - na, Do mhion bhrúigh lag mo chroí dúr leasc le
maoi-thiú ár ndearc — ndeo - - rach.

Exercises

SCALES
DOMINANT SEVENTH CHORDS and INVERSIONS
SIMILAR MOTION

Studies Nos. 20, 21 & 22

Pieces

Carolan's Concerto
(Arr. Sheila Larchet-Cuthbert)
Three Pieces for Solo Harp
(Gerard Victory)
Two Movements for Harp Duet
(Joan Trimble)

Songs

'Tis Pretty to be in Ballinderry
(Arr. Redmond Friel)
Píobaire an Mhála
(Arr. Carl Hardebec)
My Lagan Love
(Arr. Hamilton Harty)

All scales as in Ninth Lesson.

DOMINANT SEVENTH CHORD and INVERSIONS - similar motion-derived from the Dominant or Fifth note of the scale. Where possible, the upper octave is designedly used to accustom the Right Hand to the narrow space of the high position.

The playing of the Dominant Seventh differs from a common chord (Arpeggio), in that the Interval, and consequently the "spacing", varies. Whereas the intervals in the Arpeggio are of a 3rd or 4th apart, there is now a 2nd as well. Pay attention to these in order to narrow or widen the hand, as required.

B♭ MAJOR
F MAJOR
C MAJOR & C MINOR

G MAJOR & G MINOR
D MAJOR & D MINOR
A MAJOR & A MINOR

E MAJOR & E MINOR

Study No. 20

CZERNY

Study No. 21

J.P. POLE

Study No. 22

HARMONICS

M. A. C.

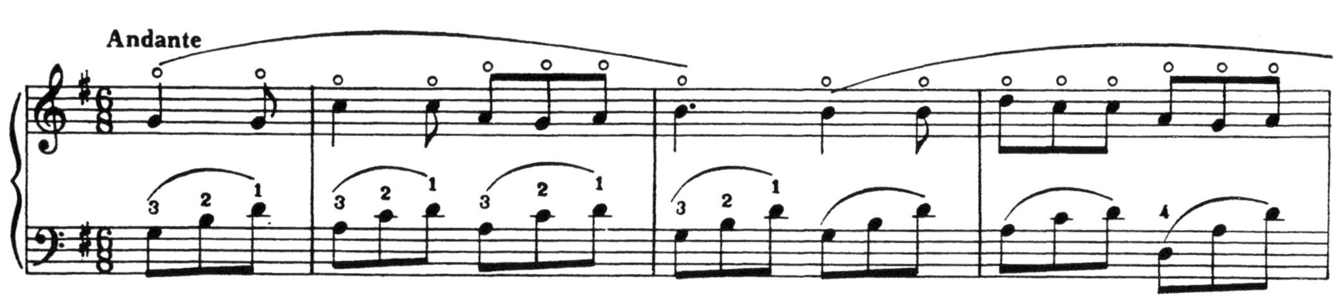

Arranged by
Sheila Larchet-Cuthbert

Carolan's Concerto

"CONCERTO" or "MRS. POWER". Presumably composed in honour of the wife of David Power of Coorheen House, on the shore of the lake of Loughrea, Co. Galway. The Italian influence of Corelli or Geminiani is very evident in this composition; in fact, a story associated with the tune tells of its being the result of a certain rivalry between Carolan and an Italian musician (who may have been Geminiani) when both were the guests of an Irish nobleman, said by one source to have been Lord Mayo.

*Play as equal notes, i.e.

Three Pieces for the Irish Harp

C, D♯, E, F, G, A, B♭

I

GERARD VICTORY

B♭s and D♯s, all others ♮

* approx. pitch glissando as indicated.

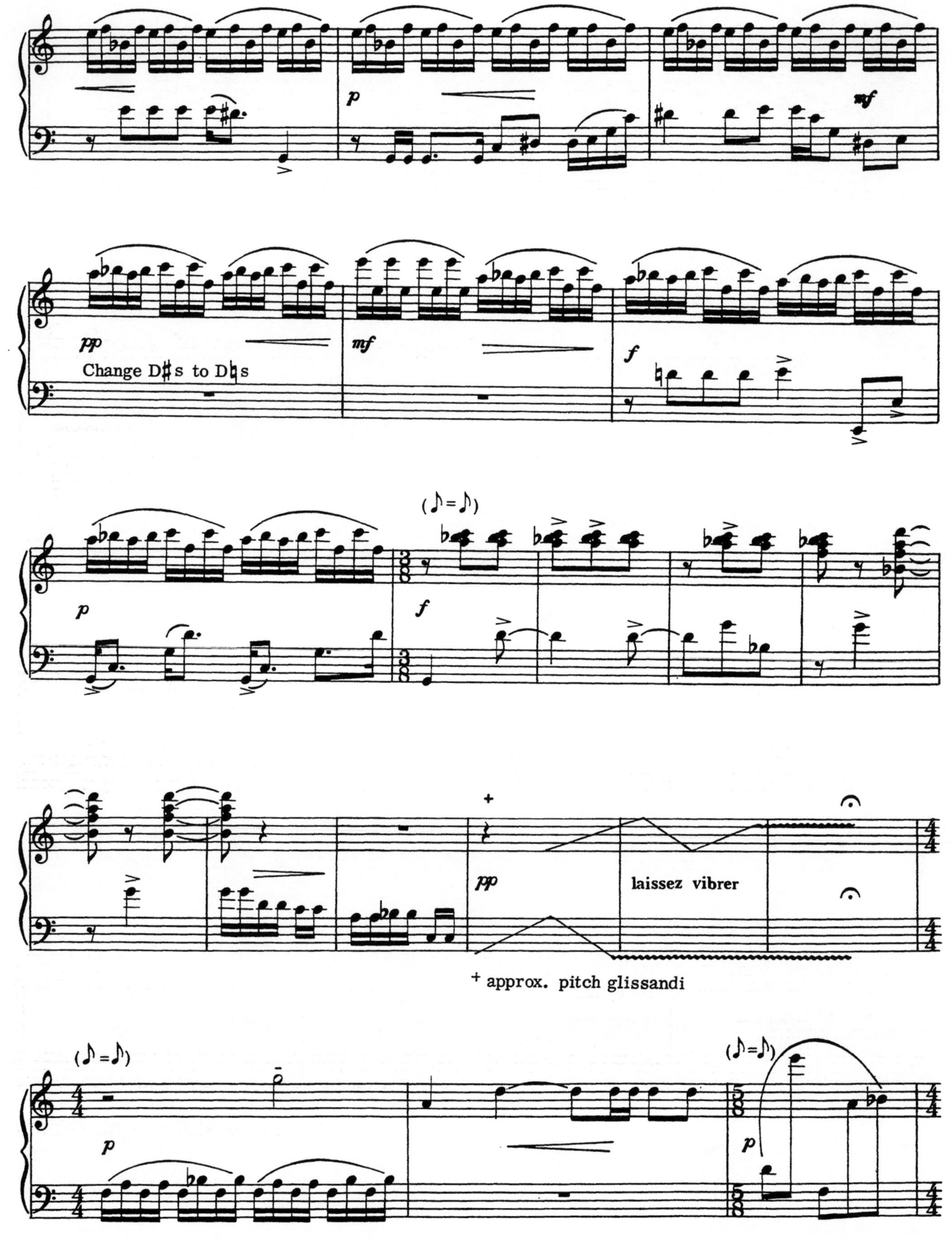

pp
Change D♯s to D♮s
mf
f
p
(♪=♪)
laissez vibrer
pp
+ approx. pitch glissandi
(♪=♪)

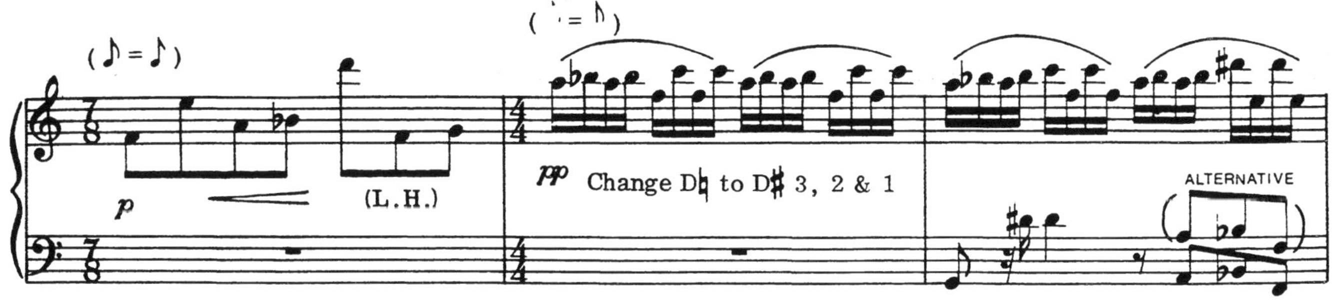

(Change only D♯(4) with B♮s and A♭s)

II

Lento Assai = Very Slow
più mosso = quicker

† Tremolo = rapid repetition of notes; thus

poco rit.
Più moto (♩= 55)
f
p
mf
6
3
poco accel.
poco rit.

(Change only B♭s and A♮s)
Also fix low F (i. e. tune down)

† approximate pitch

III

Allegro assai (♩. = 110)

f
p
f
p
RH
LH
f
f
p
f
p
RH
LH

mf
p
R.H.
L.H.
f
p
f
p
R.H.
L.H.

Presto = Very quick

Duet

JOAN TRIMBLE

ma non troppo = But not too much

più largamente = More broadly

C♮(4)
mf
p
cresc.
pp
cresc.
B♮ (2) & (3)
mp
B♭(2)
p
dim.
p
B♭(3)
pp

pp
Arioso é espressivo
mp
mp
mf
11
mf Andante
mf

triste = sadly dolce = sweetly

'Tis Pretty To Be In Ballinderry

Bunting Collection

Arranged by
REDMOND FRIEL

Sostenuto = Sustained

Píobaire an Mhála

le cead ó FHIONÁN MAC COLUIM

CARL G. HARDEBEC
a chóirigh

Allegretto scherzoso ♩. = 67

Ó's a phíob - aire an mhál___ a cás is deac - air ort.

Ó___ ró do chuir-is___ an fán ar in - íon a' tSas - an-aigh.

Suí an - seo 'rún chroí láimh liom, Ó's má chuireas an
fán uir-thi thug-as slí bheath - a di Ó
ró an - oi-read le triúr 'bheith ag siúl na
mbailte di Suí an - seo 'rún chroí láimh liom.

My Lagan Love

Words by
SEOSAMH MAC CATHMHAOIL

Arranged by
HAMILTON HARTY

Quasi senza tempo = As if (almost) without time. (i. e.) without bar-lines.

cresc.
And like a love-sick len-an-shee, She — hath my heart — in thrall;
F♮(4)
C♯(2)
f
Nor life I owe, nor lib-er-ty For Love is Lord of all.
F♯(1)
p
F♯(3)
C♮(2)
ff
pp
And of-ten when the bee-tle's horn Hath lulled — the eve to sleep,
sempre pp

I steal un - to her shie - ling lorn, And thro' the door - ing peep.
There on the crick - ets sing - ing stone She— spares the bog - wood fire,
pp
F♮(3)
C♯(3)
F♮(1)
And hums in sad sweet un - der - tone The song—— of heart's de - sire.
pp
F♯(1)
C♮(3)
F♯(3)
ppp

Exercises

Scales, Arpeggios, Inversions 2 Octaves
Contrary Motion - 1 Octave
Dominant Seventh Chord - Similar and Contrary Motion
Diminished Seventh Chord, and
Inversions - Similar Motion

Studies Nos. 23, 24 & 25

Pieces

Déirín Dé
(Éamonn Ó Gallchobhair)
Fantasia - Berceuse - Rondo
(Daniel McNulty)

Songs

Little Boats
(Arr. Herbert Hughes)
A Soft Day
(C. V. Stanford)

Harp Duet

Spanish Arch
(James Wilson)

All scales as in Ninth Lesson.

DIMINISHED SEVENTH CHORD and INVERSIONS - Similar Motion.

Because of mechnical key limitation, we cannot correctly "spell" the Diminished 7th Chord of the 3 flat scales. (See Chart, Page 16) So we begin with that of C major, etc.

Note different "spacing" as in Dominant Seventh (Page 128).

CHORD OF THE DIMINISHED SEVENTH

C MAJOR and C MINOR

AND INVERSIONS

G MAJOR and G MINOR

D MAJOR and D MINOR

A MAJOR and A MINOR

E MAJOR and E MINOR

Study No. 23

NADERMANN

Study No. 24

Study No. 25

Déirín Dé

Suantraí

ÉAMONN Ó GALLCHOBHAIR

f
rit.
p a tempo
mf
p
pp
rit.

I Fantasia

DANIEL McNULTY

R.H.
mf
dim. L.H.
p
cresc. poco a poco
f
R.H.
L.H.
mp
mf
f
B♮(2)

fz (Forzando) = Forcing, a sudden accent.

II Berceuse

Larghetto = Less slow than large

L.H.

gliss.
cresc.
gliss.

gliss.

gliss.
mf

p
mf

pp

Hands alone practice

III Rondo

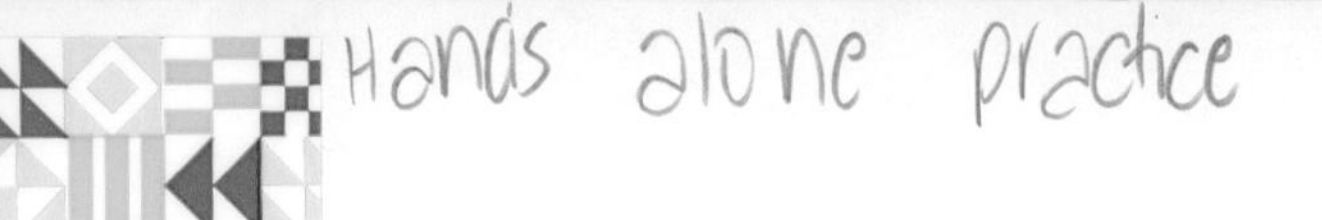

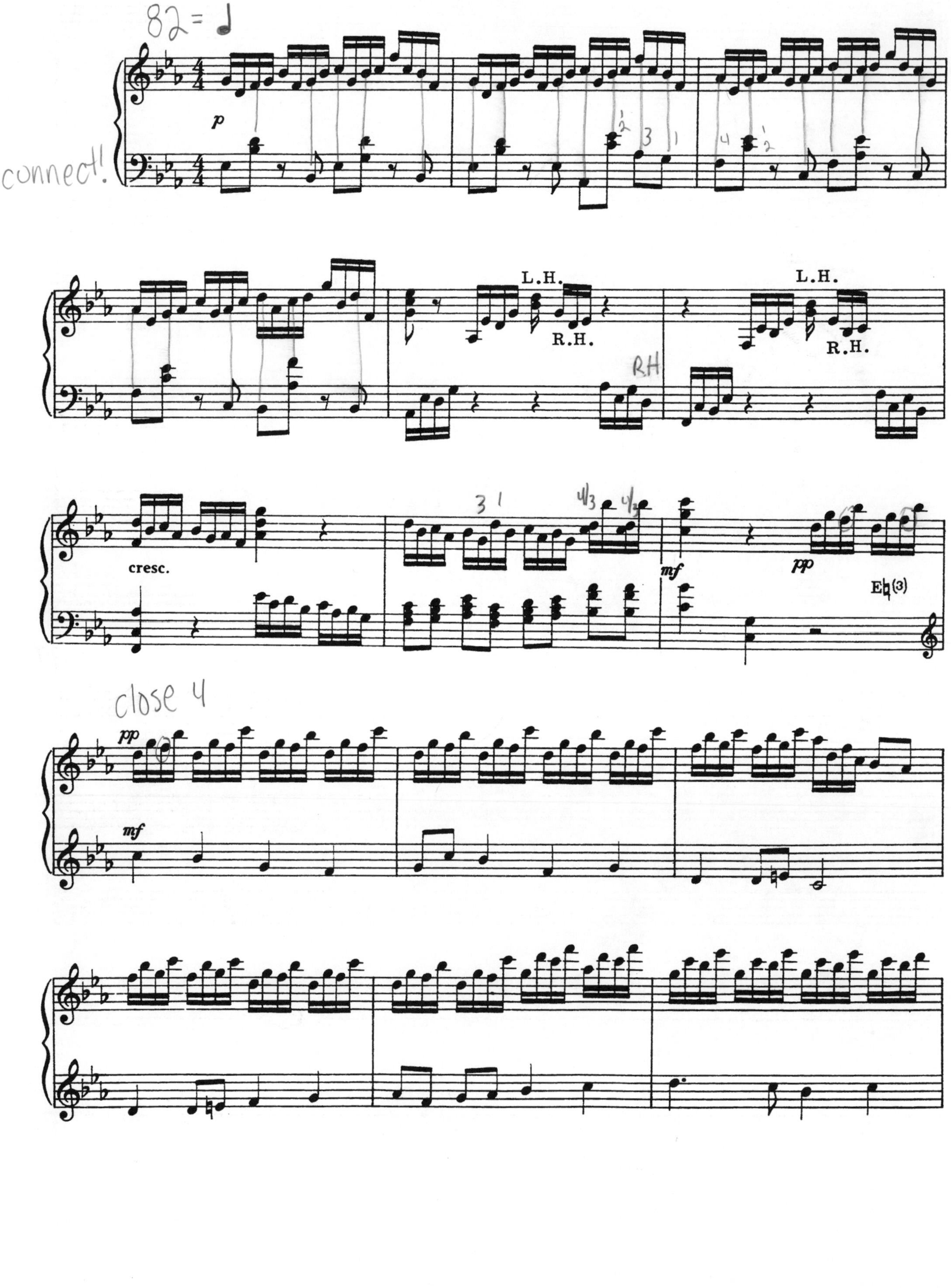
82 = ♩
p
connect!
L.H.
R.H.
RH
L.H.
R.H.
cresc.
3 1
mf
pp
E♮(3)
close 4
pp
mf

f
dim.
E♭(3)
p
L.H.
cresc.
mf

mf
mf
f
mf

poco rit.
p
L.H.
ff
f
ff
gliss.
gliss.

Words by
HAROLD BOULTON

Little Boats

Taken down from a singer at Drogheda at end of XVIII Century.

Arr. by HERBERT HUGHES

birds will be crossing the bil-lows of blue. Rock-a-by ba-by and so will you.
cresc.
dim.
F♮(4)
Troub-les are ma-ny, pleas-ures are few, But
I have a treasure while I— have you. Rock-a-by ba-by ba-loo,— ba-
cresc. F♮(3)
pp
F♯(3)
-loo.
senza rall.
ppp

A Soft Day

W.M. LETTS

C.V. STANFORD
Op. 140, No. 3

Lento moderato

mf

A soft day, thank God! A

B♮(1)

p

3 3

wind from the south—— With a hon-ey'd mouth; A scent of drench-ing leaves,

B♮(2) G♯(2)

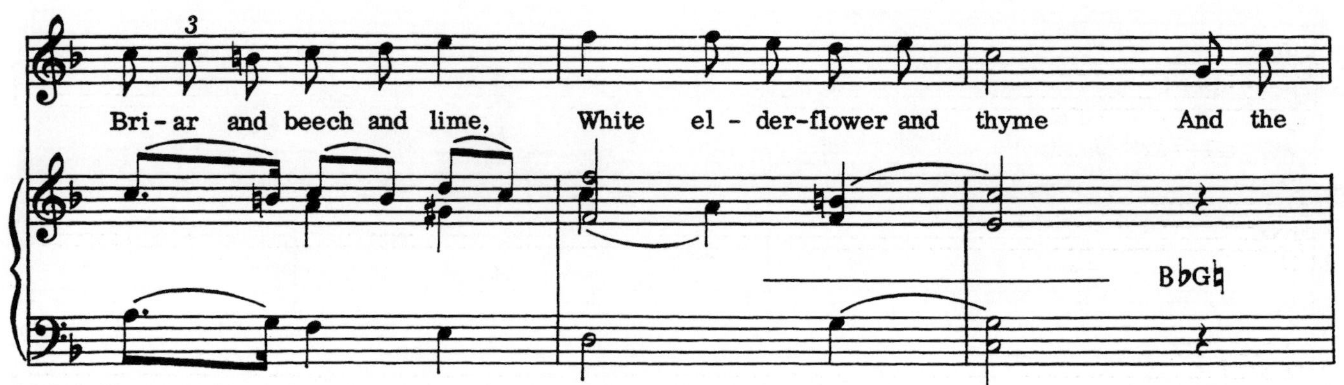

soak-ing grass smells sweet, Crushed by my two bare feet, While the
R.H.
E♭(3)
C♯(3)
rain drips, drips, drips, drips from the eaves.
C♮
E♮
p
(Damp after each chord by replacing immediately)
A soft day, thank God! The hills wear a shroud— of
E♭(3)
pp
E♮
sil-ver cloud: The web the spi-der weaves is a glitt-'ring net;
G♯(2)
B♮(2)

The wood - land path is wet,
And the soak - ing earth smells
sweet
Un - der my two bare feet,
And the
rain
drips, drips, drips, drips,
from the leaves.
G♮
B♭(2)
E♭(3)
E♮(3)
p
f rall.
3
1
2
4

Spanish Arch

JAMES WILSON

Andante malinconoso ♪ = 60ca.

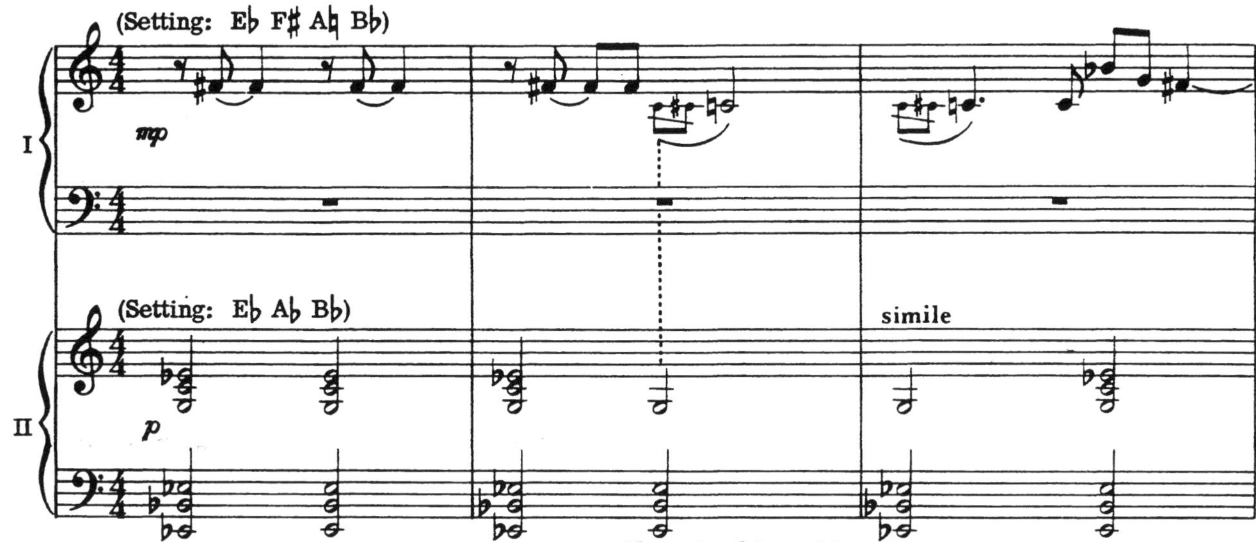

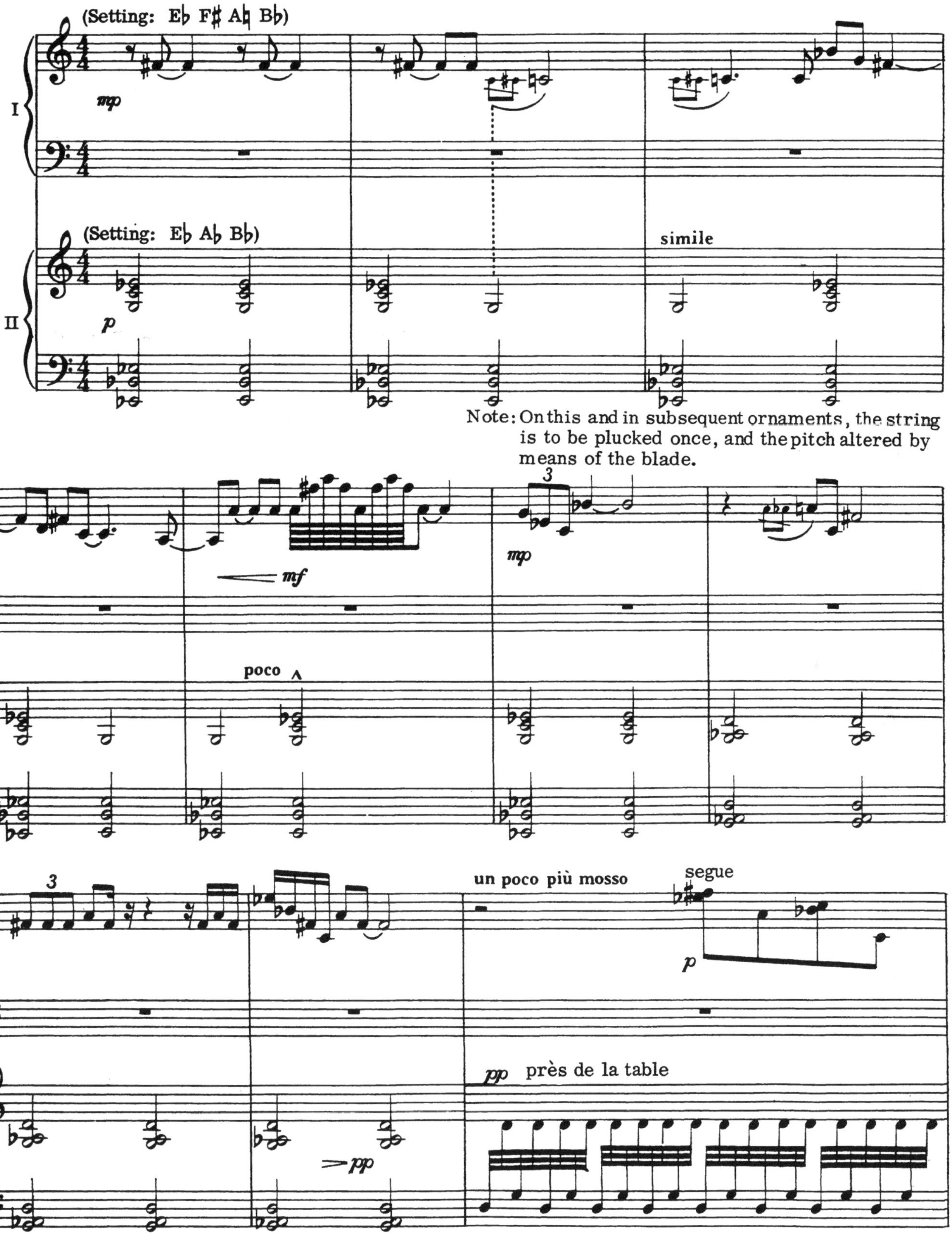
(Setting: E♭ F♯ A♮ B♭)
mp
I
(Setting: E♭ A♭ B♭)
p
II
simile
Note: On this and in subsequent ornaments, the string is to be plucked once, and the pitch altered by means of the blade.
3
mf
mp
poco
3
un poco più mosso
segue
p
pp près de la table
pp

Malinconoso = Sadly, sorrowfully.
Seque = Go on with what follows.

Près de la table (pdlt) = Near the sound board.

cresc.
poco
sf
mp
dim.
al
pp
rall.
al
Tempo primo
p
più p
pp
p naturale
f
6
dim.
f segue
(E♭ - E♮)
al
(C♮)
p
(A♮)
f
(E - E♭)

10
p
mp
(C – C♯)
pp
dim.
al
ppp
f subito
segue
(A – A♭)
12
ff
subito
poco
(F – F♯)
poco
poco
ff
12
poco
14
p
poco
poco

poco
(E – E♭)
14
poco
p
(E♮)
6
mf
segue
naturale
(E – E♭)
p
(E♭ – E♮: A – A♭)
mp
(A♭ – A♮)
(A♭ – A♮)
mf

p
(A – A♭)
segue
accel.
poco
non cresc.
p
Con moto ♩= 108
p sempre

segue
simile
poco

(E♭ - E♮)
p
mf
p
(F♯ - F♮: A♭ - A♮)
segue
f

pp subito
mf
(F - F♯)
(C♯ - C♮)
mf
cresc.
al
cresc.
p
cresc.
al
al
mf
(A♭ - A♮)

ff
ff
pp
pp
p
segue
cresc.
al
mp

(A – A♭)
pp
p
pp
segue
(C – C♯: E – E♭)
pp
pp

segue
f
simile
cresc.
f
cresc.
poco
mp subito
poco
mp subito

dim.
poco
a
poco
al
pp
poco
pp
(A – A♭: F♯ – F♮)
Tempo primo
p
naturale
(E♭ – E♮)
mp
naturale

(A♭ – A♮)
(A♭ – A♮)
mf
p
segue
pp
poco
pp
segue
naturale
poco
poco
pp

Con moto
(A – A♭)
ppp
ppp

(A♭ – A♮)
mp
mp
p
p
segue
pp
simile
pp
0

Exercises

Complete Scale Programme (all 13 keys)
Inversions of Dominant and Diminished Sevenths
Contrary Motion

Studies Nos. 26 & 27

Pieces

Étude Bitonal
(A. J. Potter)

Song

The Small Black Rose
(Arr. John F. Larchet)

for Two Harps

Two Sketches
(Brian Boydell)
Scintillae
(Seoirse Bodley)

Quintet

A Carolan Tune
for Harp and String Quartet
(Havelock Nelson)

Complete Scale Programme as in Eleventh Lesson.

CHORD of the DOMINANT and DIMINISHED SEVENTH in CONTRARY MOTION with INVERSIONS.

Note "spacing" as page 128. Now the intervals vary between the hands.

DOMINANT and DIMINISHED SEVENTH CHORDS

E♭ MAJOR

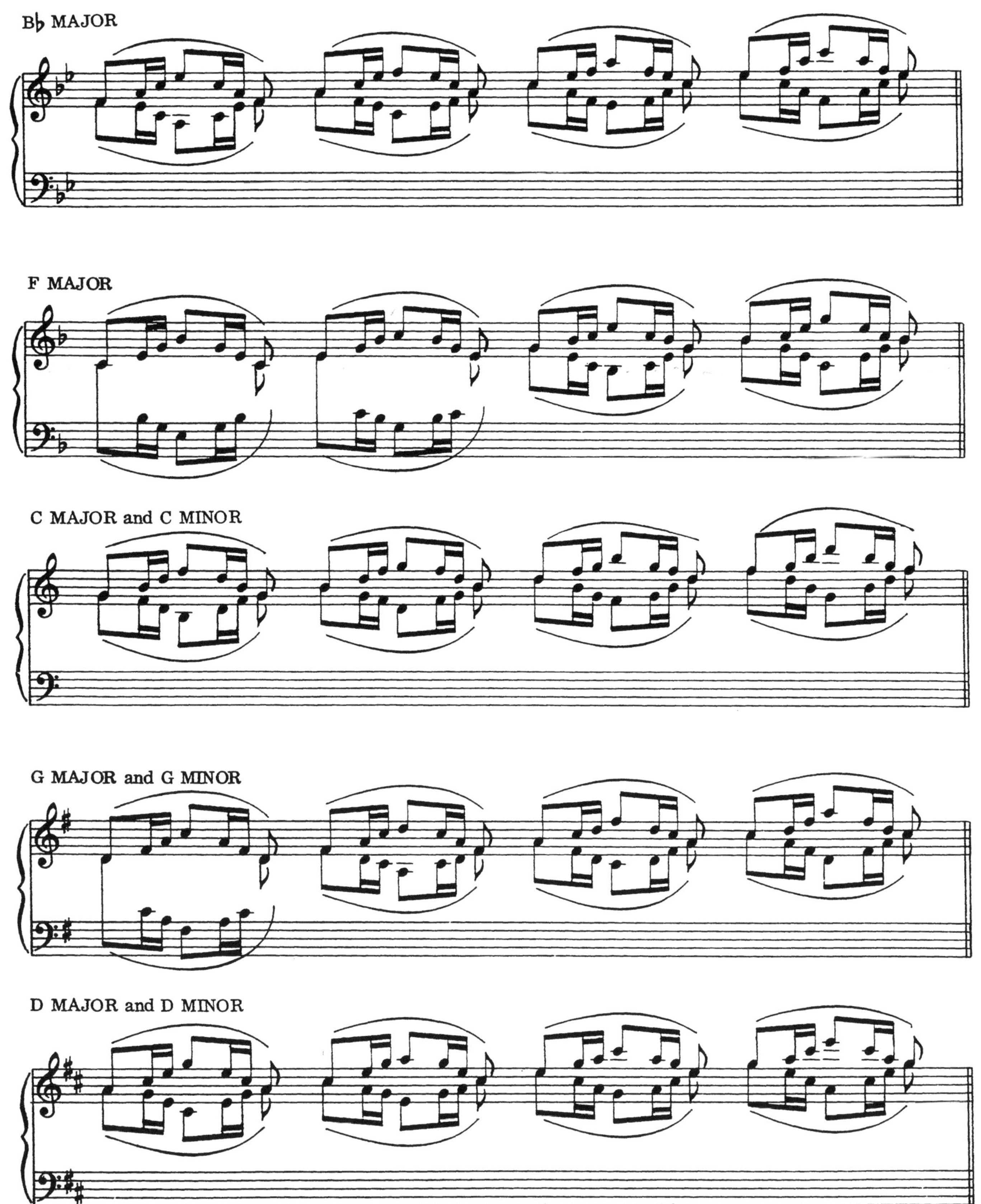
B♭ MAJOR
F MAJOR
C MAJOR and C MINOR
G MAJOR and G MINOR
D MAJOR and D MINOR

INVERSIONS - CONTRARY MOTION in all POSSIBLE KEYS

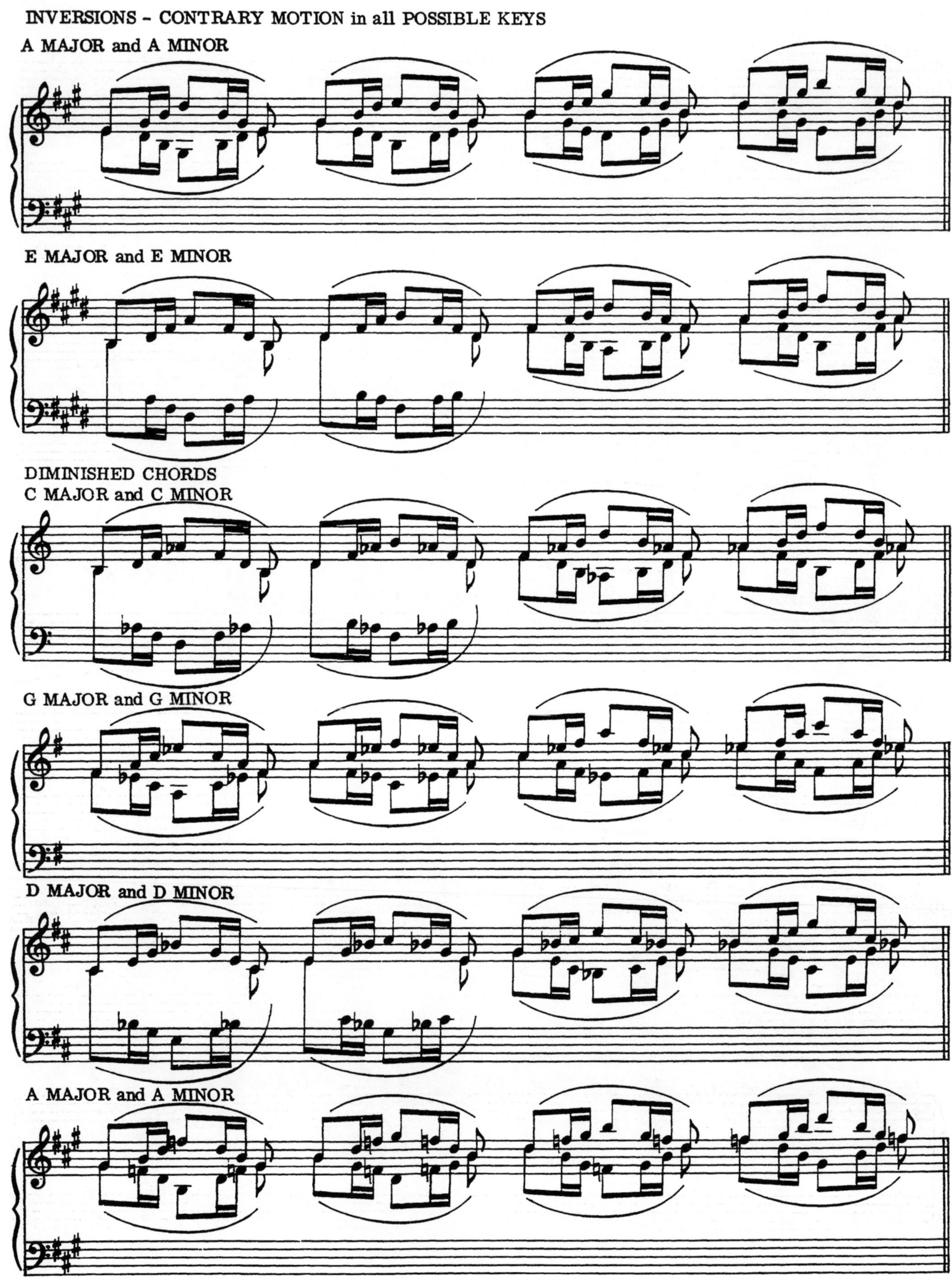

Study No. 26
NADERMAN
Allegro

KRUMPHOLTZ

Moderato

Étude Bitonal

for E♭ Harp

A.J. POTTER

Note: Tune upper notes as follows:
(i.e. raise them with blades)

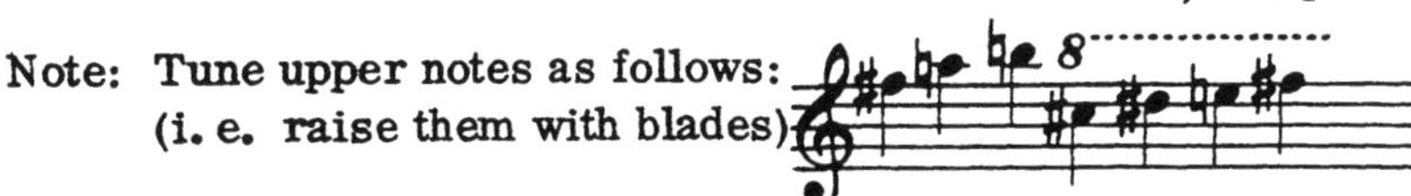

Adagio ♪ = 60
sempre con rubato

p f
sempre simile
rit.
calando
lunga
rit.
LV
segue

Vivace 𝅗𝅥 = 76

f sf

Vivace = quick, lively

Calando = decreasing both tone and speed.

Lunga = long.

LV (Laisser Vibrer) = allow to vibrate.

Ten. (Tenuto) = Held

The Small Black Rose

Words by
DONAL O'SULLIVAN

Arranged by
JOHN F. LARCHET

Con anima = With deep feeling
Agitato = Agitated
Dolente = Sadly

mf
3. I a - dore thee, watch o'er thee the
4. I'd roam in the gloam - ing through
mf
live- - long year, With no guer-don for love's bur - den but black de -
Mun - ster's plain, Ov - er hill side and by rill side her heart to
G♯
spair; With spirits pi - ning, health de - cli - ning, my pass - ion grows, Yet
gain; She is fair - er, far ra - rer, than an-y flower that glows, Is she
mp
G♮ F♯(3)
f
F♮
B♭(3) mp
3rd verse
4th verse
vain - ly I strive to gain thee, my Small Black Rose.
yield-ing to my plead - ing, my Small Black Rose.
B♮
f
f

mf Agitato
5. The sea's flood will be— blood-red, the
ff
Agitato
B♭(2)
sky— a - flame. The whole world will be— hurled in - to— ruin— and
G♯
f
a Tempo
shame, Hills will trem-ble and crum-ble in— ag - - ony's throes, - Ere the
p
G♮ F♯(3)
f
D♯ F♮
D♮
B♭(3) p
a Tempo
Dolente e Decrescendo
day that death takes— thee, my Small— Black Rose!
B♮
pp
Dolente e Decrescendo

Dance for an Ancient Ritual

BRIAN BOYDELL

mf
change
p
mp
mp
mf
mp
mf
mf
mf espr.
p
change
mf

dim.
change
p
mp
dim.
change
p
change
mp
p

p mp p mp p mp mp

8 gliss. mp pp p

mp pp p

pp rall. 0 0 Both harmonics

rall. 0 0 0 0 0

No. 2 of Four Pieces for Two Irish Harps

BRIAN BOYDELL

♩ = c. 60

Throughout range

Except

Except

Throughout range

p mf p pp mp mf ff ff

8

loco
mp
p
mp
p
p
p
pp
f
ff
ff

change
loco
rit.
a tempo
mp
change
f
p
change
loco
dim.
pp
mp

p
mf
pp
5
mp
p
mp
rit.
ff
pp
cresc.
f
sempre glissando
mf
mp
p
p
dim.
p

sempre
diminuendo
pp
p
mp espr.
pp
mp
p
rallentando
p
pp

Duet - Scintillae

SEÓIRSE BODLEY

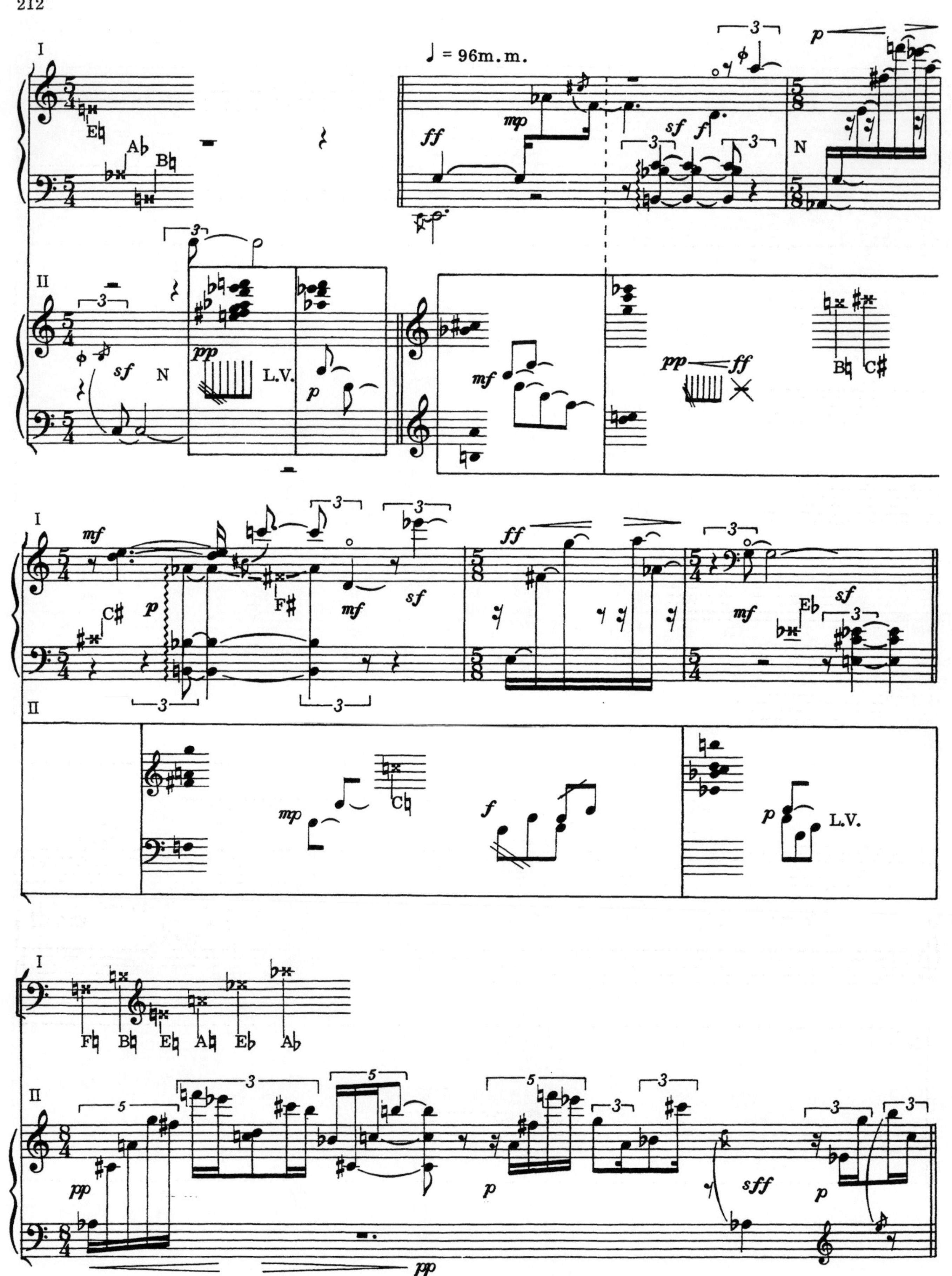
I
♩ = 96m.m.
E♮
A♭
B♮
N
II
N
L.V.
B♮
C♯
I
C♯
F♯
E♭
II
C♮
L.V.
I
F♮
B♮
E♮
A♮
E♭
A♭
II

I

pp

sf

sf

p

sf

C♮

pp

p

II

sf

E♮

F♮

p

A♮

pp

I
II
L.V.

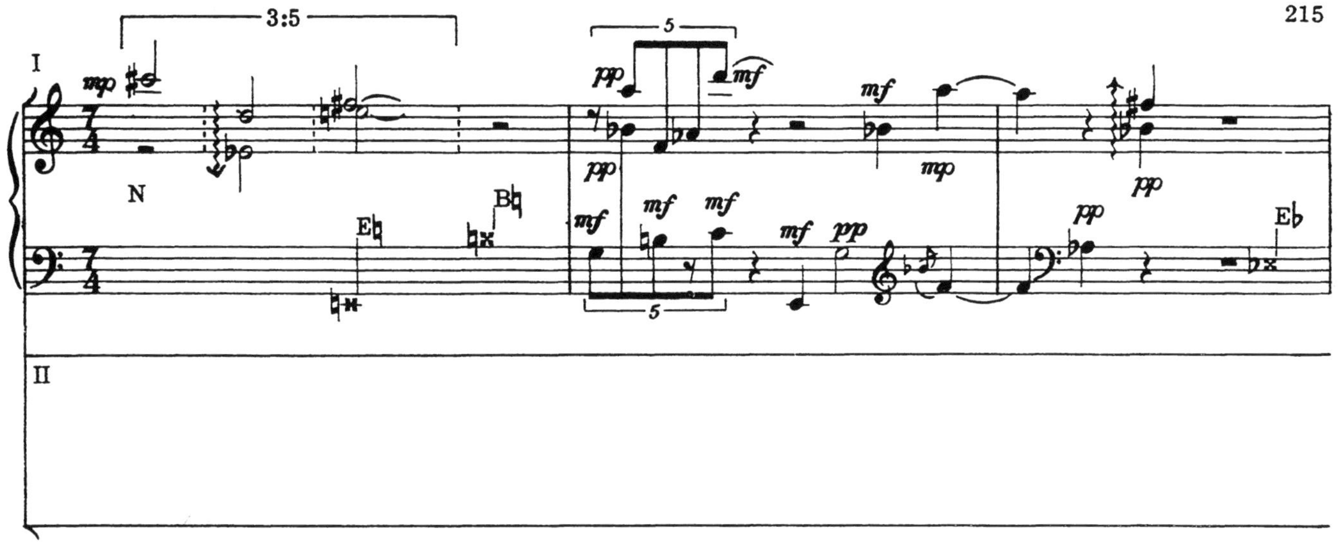
3:5
I
mp
N
E♮
B♮
5
pp
mf
pp
mf
mf
mf
mp
mf
pp
pp
pp
E♭
II

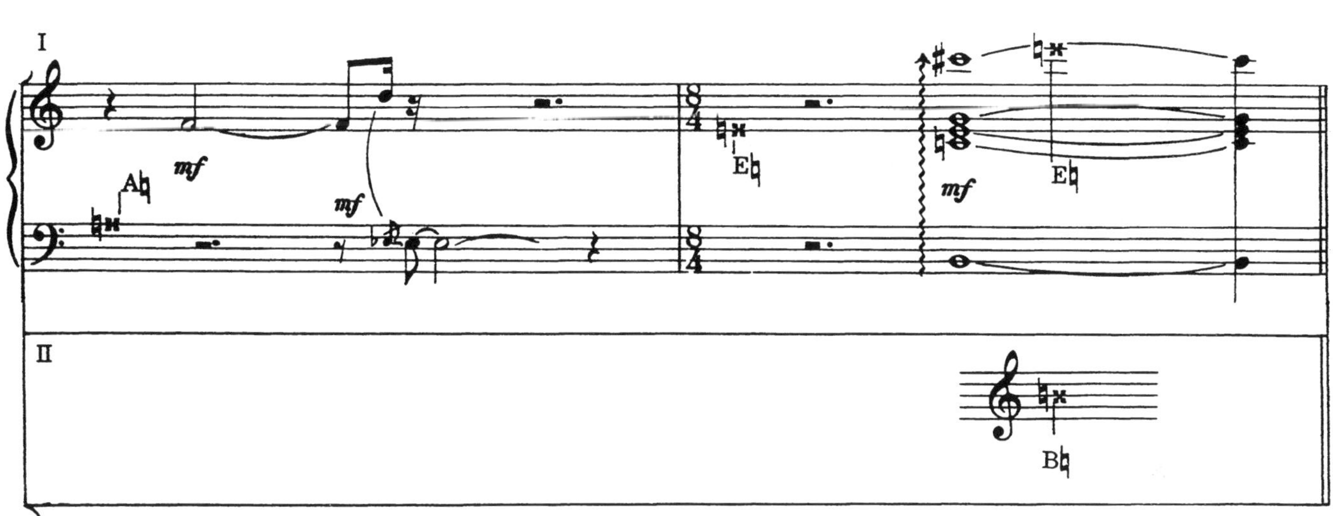
I
A♮
mf
mf
E♮
mf
E♮
II
B♮

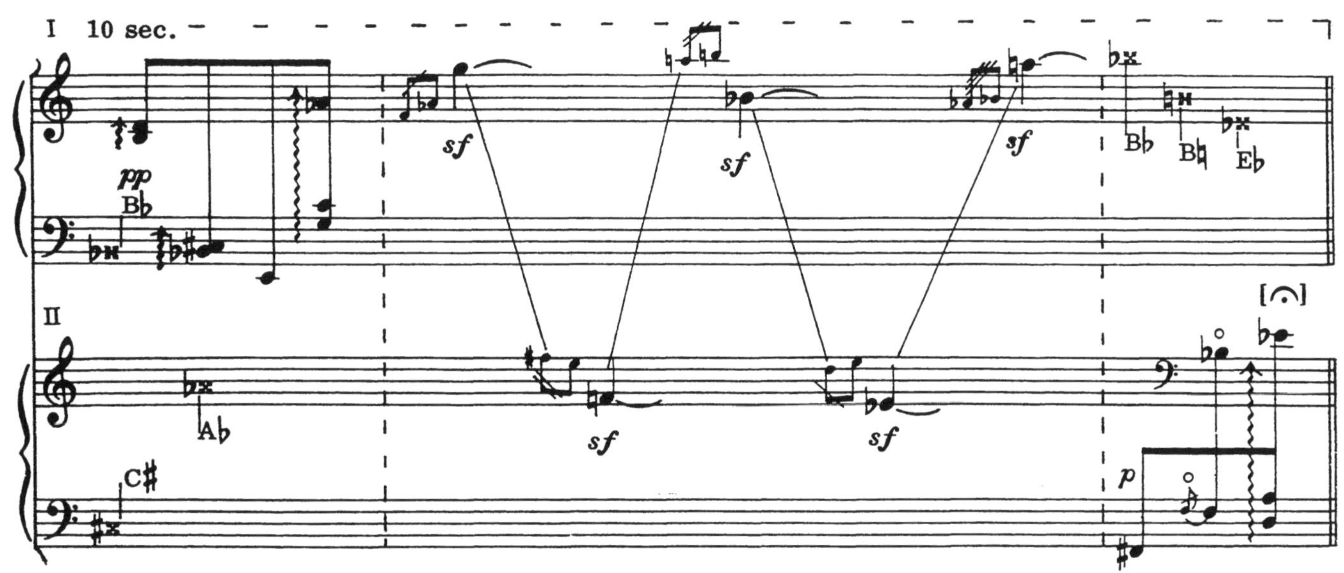
I 10 sec.
pp
B♭
sf
sf
sf
B♭
B♮
E♭
II
A♭
C♯
sf
sf
p

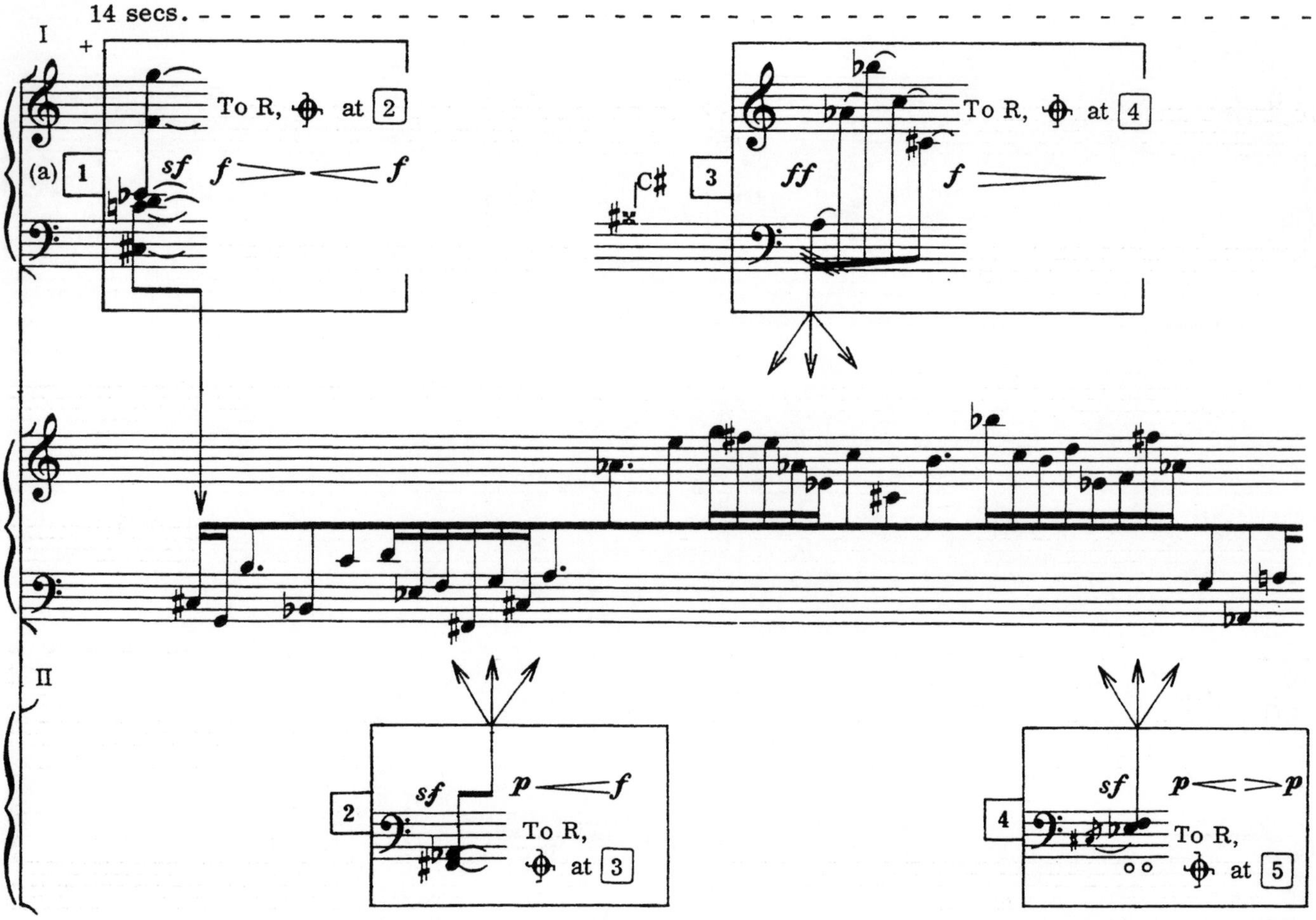

14 secs.

I

\+

(a) 1 sf f f
To R, at 2

C♯
3 ff f
To R, at 4

*R

II

2 sf p f
To R, at 3

4 sf p p
To R, at 5

*R = reservoir (a) [1], [2] etc. = order of entries.

+Play [1] then to R, damp at entry [2], Play [2] then to R (at indicated dynamics always) etc.

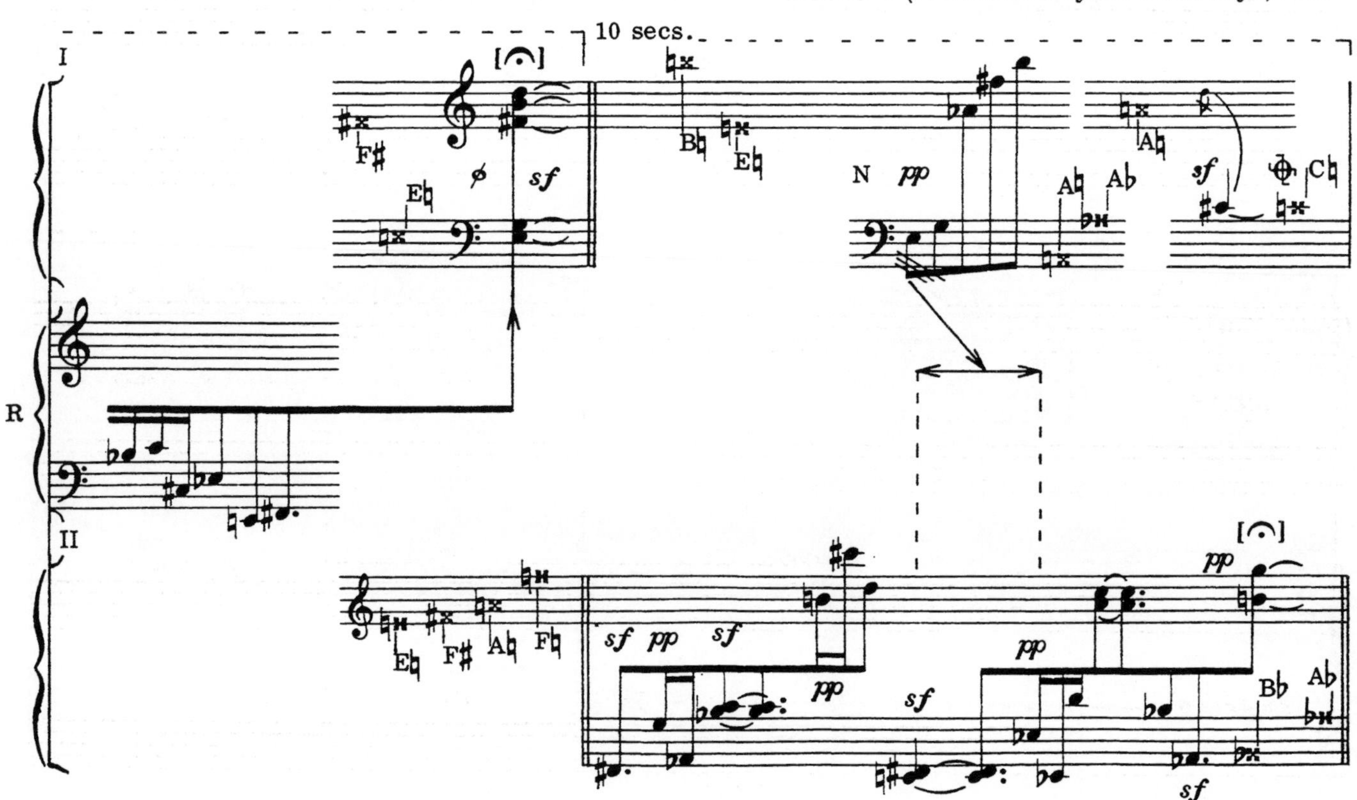

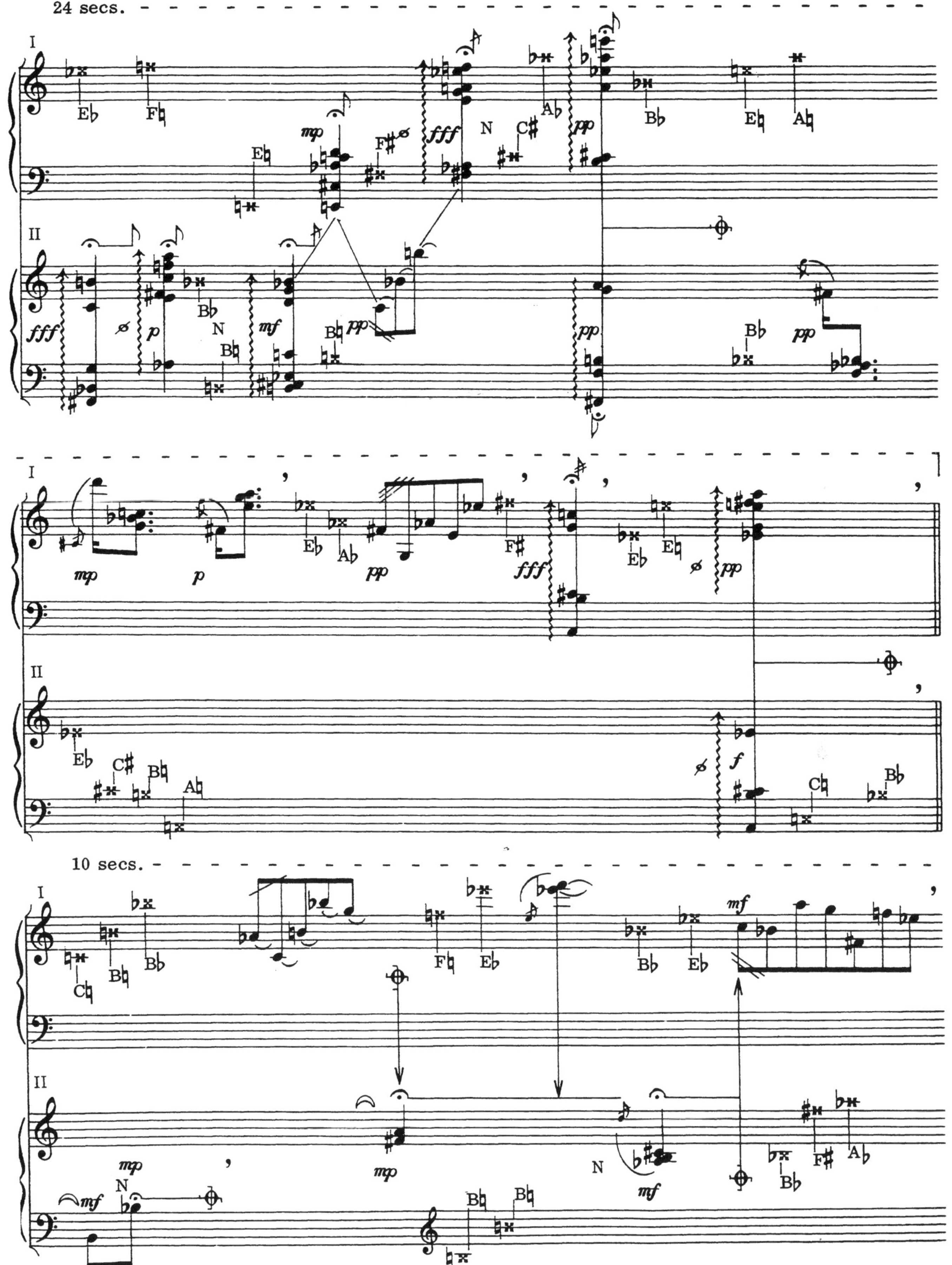
24 secs.
I
II
10 secs.
I
II

* etc. = 5 hand positions between and . Strike as hard as possible with the palm of the hand.

I
II
♩ = 58m.m.
♩ = 67m.m.
Eb
Ab
C#
C
Ah
E
F#
F
B
N
(N)

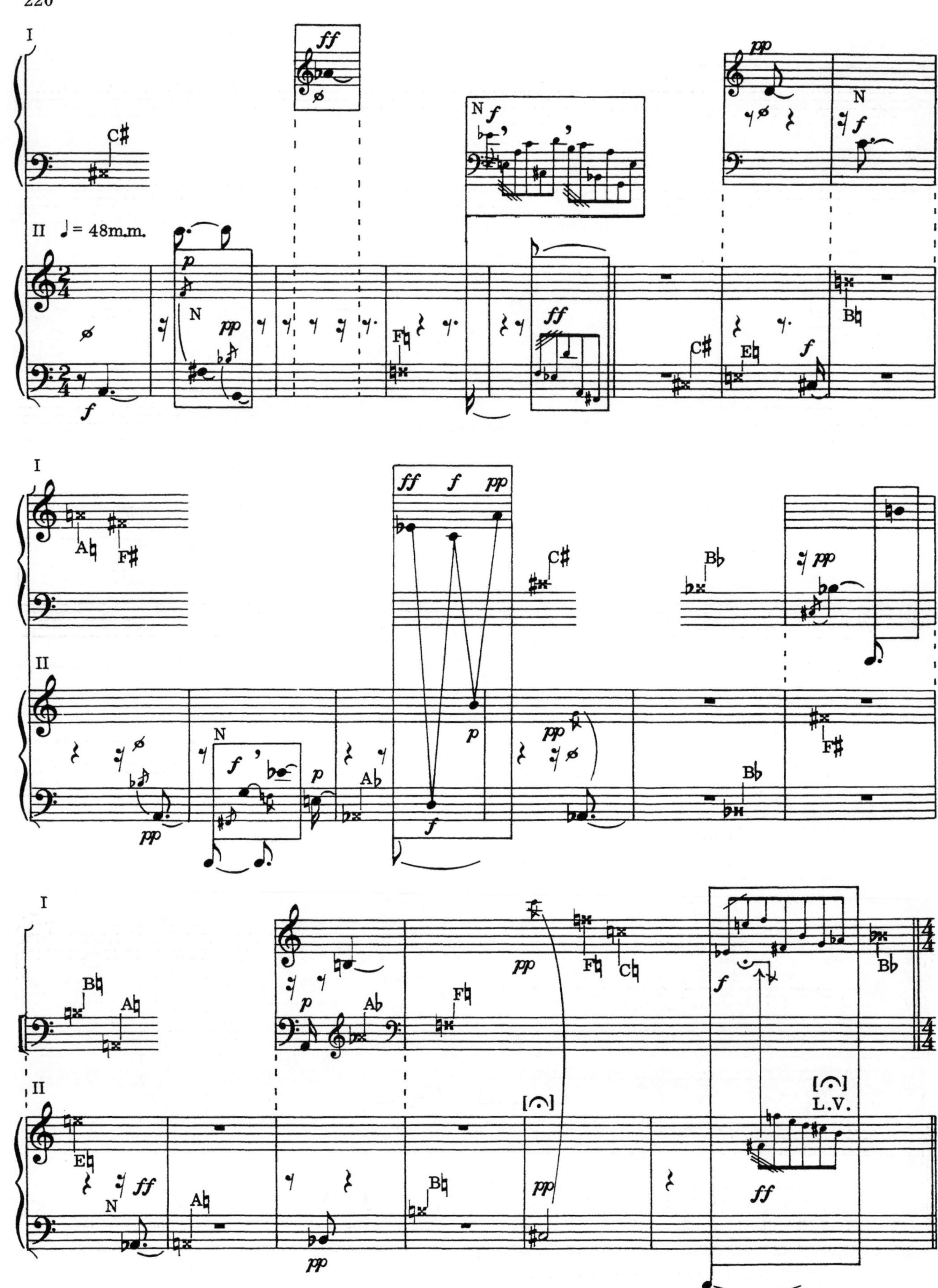
I
II
♩ = 48m.m.
N
[𝄐]
L.V.

I
♩ = 139m.m.
L.V.
pp cresc.
ff
II
F♮
E♭
A♮
C♮
B♮
N

81m.m.

12 secs.

82m.m.

TABLE

(1) All accidentals refer only to the note to which they are prefixed.

(2) A♮ etc = Alteration of indicated string.

(3) = Play all the notes within the indicated range.

(4) = Fast; = faster; = faster still.

(5) = Pluck with fingernails.

(6) ϕ = Près de la table.

Quintet
A Carolan Tune

Arranged
HAVELOCK NELSON

arco
A
mf
arco
mf
arco
mf
arco
mf
A
f
pp

pp
pp
B
f
f
f
f
B

dim. – e – rall.
dim. – e – rall.
dim. – e – rall.
dim. – e – rall.
rall.
Andante
pp
pp
pp
pp
mp (cantabile)
Andante
mp
p

mp
p
mp
mp
mf
p
pizz.
pizz.

arco
pp
poco rit.
C
p
pp
arco
poco rit.
p
pp
pp
poco rit.
p
p
pp
poco rit.
p
pp
C
poco rit.
p
p
p
p

Vivace ma non troppo
Vivace ma non troppo
f
f
f
f
f
mf
gliss.

D
D
gliss.
f
mp
p
p
mp

pp
E
f
f
f
f
E
mf
gliss.

p
p
p
p
gliss.
gliss.
ff
ff
ff
ff
ff
gliss.

MAINTENANCE

The care of your harp is of the utmost importance. Any instrument will deteriorate if it is not looked after.

PLACING: When not using it (or even while practising) do not place the harp near a fire-grate, an open window or in a draught. It is affected by all the atmospheric changes of heat, cold or damp and the strings expand and contract accordingly.

When not using it, do not leave the harp standing on a playing stool, but place in a corner (neck-piece towards the wall) for safety. The harp will not fall forward but is very easily tipped back.

STRINGING: When replacing a string it is advisable to double-knot the new string around a thicker piece of gut, cut to about 1.5 inches in length. (A 4th octave string or cello string is useful for this purpose.) In this way, the knots are not crushed and the string has a longer life – a very important consideration, as strings are an expensive item for a harpist! For reasons of economy, it is also advisable not to cut the unused section of a new string for at least two weeks to give it time to stretch. Cutting the string too soon can be a very wasteful practice.

It is necessary to have a reserve set of strings which are best kept in a tin or box. The wire strings naturally last thc longest, but if one should break, be careful not to lose the tiny disc which holds it in place at the back of the soundboard.

Finally, *never* leave blades in an 'on' position when the harp is not in use. This will wear out the strings sooner. For information on ordering and purchase of strings, see chart, page 7. Strings should be named by 'octave' number rather than by pitch, e.g. 3rd octave C rather than middle C.

CARRYING: When transporting the harp, *do not* carry it by the fore-pillar as this will place undue stress on this carefully balanced section. Rather divide its weight between both hands, the right holding a section of the back-piece and the left *on* the fore-pillar. Most harps are equipped with an outer travelling cover with a handle well placed to achieve a good balance.

WHEN PLAYING: Concert halls and stages have notoriously variable temperatures. Therefore, always allow sufficient time to acclimatize your harp to the change of atmosphere. In other words, be prepared for much tuning and give the strings time to settle down.

THREE EPOCHS IN THE HISTORY OF THE IRISH HARP

'The harp is one of the oldest instruments in the world. We know nothing about its remote origin and very little about the origin of the European harps, including the Irish form. 'Cruit' – the Irish word for harp – must originally have meant not a harp, but a lyre. It is possible that the harp was brought to Ireland by the invading Danes in the 9th century.' (Joan Rimmer, *The Irish Harp*)

PRE-CELTIC

CELTIC-CHRISTIAN

NORSE

9th Century	Appearance of fully-framed triangular harp.
9th or 10th Century	Depictions of harps on Irish crosses including Kells. Clonmacnoise, Kinitty, Monasterboice, etc.

NORMAN

12th Century	Irish harpers enjoy high reputation in Europe.
14th Century	'Trinity College' Harp dates from this time.

TUDOR

16th Century	The harp as a distinctive symbol of Ireland was introduced on the coinage by Henry VIII around 1526.
17th Century	The Flight of the Earls in 1607 and end of the old Gaelic order. Harpers of this period – Rory Dall Ó Catháin (died about 1653), Cornelius Lyons and David Murphy.

'Unfortunately, the arts of the reciters and of the harpers in poetry, songs, eulogies and satires have passed away without record.'(Joan Rimmer, *The Irish Harp*)

18th and 19th Century The Age of the Itinerant Harper

Many of them were blind, like Turlough O'Carolan. They lived the hard life of a musical 'commercial traveller', going on horseback from one gentleman's house to another playing Irish music and sometimes composing it too. O'Carolan was the last of the harper-composers (1670-1738).

1792 In an attempt to revive the ancient art of harp-playing, the Belfast Harp Meeting was held and Edward Bunting was engaged to note down the tunes played. Of the ten players who attended, only one used the old 'nail' method. He was Denis Hempson (blind) of Co. Derry and was aged 97 years. The other nine players were as follows:

Arthur O'Neill (blind) of Co. Tyrone, aged 58
Charles Fanning of Co. Cavan, aged 56
Daniel Black (blind) of Co. Derry, aged 75
Charles Byrne of Co. Leitrim, aged 80
Hugh Higgins (blind) of Co. Mayo, aged 55
Patrick Quin of Co. Armagh, aged 47
William Carr of Co. Armagh, aged 15
Rose Mooney (blind) of Co. Meath, aged 52
James Duncan of Co. Down, aged 45

Many played the music of O'Carolan.

'This attempt to revive the harp was unsuccessful. The 18th century harpers, already archaic and somewhat anachronistic, could not adapt to the 19th century. By the end of that century's second decade, the old Irish harp was gone.' (Joan Rimmer, *The Irish Harp*)

In Dublin, John Egan and his nephew and successor produced the 'portable harp' about 1819. This harp was equipped with seven thumb levers set in the fore-pillar and was in effect a small single-action 'handle' harp. Thomas Moore used one to accompany himself when singing his 'Irish Melodies'. Perhaps Egan was attempting to compete with Erard's single action development, but it proved in the end no more than a passing fashion.

'There seems to have been little harp-playing in Ireland, apart from the visits of foreign virtuosi on the pedal harp, after the third decade of the nineteenth century.' (Joan Rimmer, *The Irish Harp*)

1902 James MacFall produced the 'Tara harp'.

EUROPEAN DEVELOPMENT

1792 Sebastian Erard produced his first single action pedal harp in London (having fled there from Paris during the French Revolution).

1794 Erard produced a greatly improved version.

1810 Sebastian Erard now produced his double action harp. This model continued to be developed by his nephew, Pierre.

TODAY – THE 21ST CENTURY

The Irish harp now enjoys a new-found popularity, but its revival is entirely contemporary. The technique is largely derived from that of the pedal harp and in no way seeks to recreate the ancient style of playing. The Irish harp can now take its place wherever music is played, be it amongst traditional musicians on the concert platform, or even in the world of entertainment.

'Different as it is from its historic predecessor, it has a justifiable place in the re-creation for twentieth-century audiences of music from the time when the old Irish harp, with its willow sound-box and brass strings, was in its heyday.'
(Joan Rimmer, *The Irish Harp*)

BIOGRAPHY

Harpers

Harper-Composers

Hempson, Dennis (1695-1807)
He was born in County Derry and his life spanned three centuries. He died at Magilligan at the age of 112 years, retaining his mental faculties to the end and playing the harp, on which he was a great performer, the day before his death. He acquired great fame as an exponent of the old Irish harp technique, showing himself master of an astonishing variety of effects.

Lyons, Cornelius
Born in Co. Kerry. Harper to the Earl of Antrim.
A contemporary of O'Carolan, Lyons was an arranger of variations on Airs such as 'Eibhlín a Rún' and 'An Cúileann'.

Murphy, David
Harper to Lord Mayo and a contemporary of O'Carolan. An accomplished player and poet, he composed 'Tiarna Mhaigh Eó' about 1717.

O'Carolan, Turlough (1670-1738)
Born in County Meath. He was the last of the Irish harper-composers and the only one whose pieces have survived in any number: about two hundred are extant. O'Carolan was blinded by smallpox in early youth and adopted music as a career. His genius for making melody manifested itself almost at once and for nearly fifty years he travelled the Irish countryside, staying at the great houses and entertaining the company with his playing and singing. The great majority of his pieces were composed in honour of his patrons and in most cases he devised verses to fit the music. He was also a familiar figure in Dublin, where he must have heard the music of Corelli, Vivaldi and Geminiani. The influence of Corelli can be discerned in the form and melodic idiom of a number of his compositions. At the end of his life he returned to the home of his aged patroness, Mrs MacDermott Roe at Alderford, County Leitrim, composed his last piece 'Farewell to Music', and died shortly afterwards.

Ó CATHÁIN, RORY DALL
Born in Co. Derry. One of the greatest of the Ulster harpers, who, after the downfall of Hugh O'Neill, resided principally in Scotland. He played before James VI of that Kingdom (James I of England) and died about 1650, at Castle Eglinton, in extreme old age.

HARPIST CONTRIBUTORS

BOLGER, MERCEDES GARVEY, ARCM
Began studying cello at four and harp at fourteen. Studied at RIAM, UCD, and RCM, London. Having played one season as Cellist and Second Harpist with Scottish National Orchestra, she returned to Dublin to play as Principal Harpist and Soloist with the (then) RTÉLO and later with the RTÉSO. Has made recordings of Irish music in Holland, Germany, Belgium and Switzerland and was Professor of harp in the RIAM for some years. Co-editor with Gráinne Yeats of *Sounding Harps*, a series of books for Irish harp. Co-editor with Elizabeth Hannon of *My Gentle Harp*. These books are published by Cairde na Cruite of which Mercedes is a founder member.

CALTHORPE, NANCY (1914-1998)
A native of Waterford, from a family of professional musicians. Commenced musical training at very early age, eventually obtaining teacher's LRAM and LTCL in Instrumental and Vocal studies. Began teaching career in Ursuline Convent, Sligo. Later taught in Loreto Abbey, Rathfarnham, and Dominican Convent, Sion Hill, where she was Music Lecturer in Froebel Training College. In 1966 was awarded an Oireachtas Prize for the setting of three Irish Songs with Irish Harp Accompaniment. Adjudicated at all leading Irish Feiseanna. Member of teaching staff of College of Music, Dublin, for a number of years, teaching piano, singing, harmony, aural training and Irish harp. Published several books of arrangements of traditional melodies for Irish harp

CROWLEY, ANNE, ARIAM, B. MUS. (-1978)
Studied organ with Aloys Georg Fleischmann in Cork and piano, singing and composition in the RIAM in Dublin. Gold medallist for organ and Irish harp. Studied concert harp with Mercedes Bolger and Maria Korchinska. Taught Irish harp in the RIAM.

MCGRATH, MERCEDES BOLGER (1894-1980)
Commenced violin and piano at the RIAM with Madeleine Larchet and Margaret O'Hea. Continued violin in London with Dettmar Dressel. Studied in Dresden for a year with Rudolph Bastich, Deputy Leader of the Opera House Orchestra. Studied harmony and attended orchestral classes at the Conservatorium. Heard all the leading opera singers and most famous violinists of the day. On returning to Dublin, continued at the RIAM under Simonnetti and Esposito and took an honours degree at the NUI under Dr Charles Kitson. Later became interested in the Irish harp and its history, in Irish traditional music, and also in the revival of Church Music. Founded, and conducted for nine years, the Gorey Operatic Society.

MERVYN, RUTH, LRAM.
Scholarship holder at Brighton School of Music. Came to live in Ireland (Belfast) 1935 and subsequently moved to Co. Donegal. Organist and teacher of piano. Winner of composer's competitions at Port Stewart, Derry, Sligo, Limerick and Dundalk. Gold medallist in composition at Dublin Feis Ceoil and prizewinner for composition at Oireachtas.

NI CHORMAIC, TREASA BROE

Described by Mrs. Bolger as 'the real descendant of the old harpers'. Her first harp was found in a bog and she was taught to play by her father. Later she obtained an Erard on which she mostly played her larger repertoire of traditional music. 'I don't think she had any further training but she was intensely musical, with a wonderful ear and excellent taste.' Mrs. Bolger continues: 'Everything she played was arranged by herself, with the exception of a couple of arrangements made for her by the late Joseph Crofts. On one occasion she played at the St. Patrick's Day Concert at the Queen's Hall in London and literally brought the house down with her rendering of Brian Boru's March. I succeeded in taking down some of her arrangements, including the March, and some were published by Pigotts. She had many pupils.'

NÍ SHEAGHDA, MÁIRÍN (BEAN UÍ FEIRITÉIR) (1913–1990)

Born in Dublin. Educated in Scoil Bhríghde and Dominican Convent, Eccles Street, Dublin. Graduate of UCD. Feis Ceoil and Feis Maitiú Cup winner and gold medallist for singing and harp. Medals for singing and harp at Feiseanna throughout the country and subsequently adjudicator. Taught singing in Irish colleges during summer sessions. Deeply indebted to harp teacher, Caroline Townshend. Represented Ireland as harpist in Celtic countries and USA. Played at ICA World Congress in London. Lectured to NUI Club, London, during first Tóstal, 1953. Member of staff, Dominican Convent, Sion Hill, Dublin, teaching harp and other subjects. Pupils internationally known on radio and television. Founder-member of Cairde na Cruite.

NÍ SHEAGHDA, RÓISÍN (BEAU UÍ THUAMA), BA (Celtic Studies). H.Dip. in Ed. (UCD)

Music course under J.F. Larchet. Studied piano in RIAM. Studied harp with Caroline Townshend. Gold medallist for Irish Traditional Singing and singing to own harp accompaniment at Oireachtas, Feis Maitiú and Feis Ceoil (Townshend Cup). Delegate lecturer and harper-singer at International and Inter-Celtic Congresses in Brittany, Wales, Cornwall, Isle of Man, Scotland and France, 1939-69. Well-known performer on radio and television. Indebted to parents, Seán and Caitlín Ó Seaghdha, and to the late Fionán MacColuim and Colm Ó Lochlainn for encouraging her interest in and appreciation of Irish music.

TOWNSHEND, CAROLINE

A gifted musician, both as a pianist and player of the Irish harp. For many years she lived at Glandore, Co. Cork. Interested in Irish language, music and culture. Taught the Irish harp to a wide range of students near her home. On moving to Dublin, she taught quite advanced musicians such as Sanchia Pielou, the Ní Sheaghda sisters and many others. The late Denis McCullough made a number of harps at her request, one of which was modelled on the Brian Boru harp. Presented a cup to the Feis Ceoil for the singing of two songs in Irish to one's own accompaniment on the Brian Boru harp.

YEATS, GRÁINNE

Born Dublin. Educated Scoil Bhríghde, Alexandra College, TCD (BA History). Musical education RIAM and College of Music in piano, singing and harp. Daughter of historian, P.S. Ó hÉigeartaigh. Member of Dowland Consort. A distinguished performer, she has toured extensively in Europe and America, winning wide acclaim for her ability to blend harp and voice into a uniquely satisfying art form. In 1966, she received the Harriet

Cohen International Award for solo instruments. Her research interests include the early wire-strung harp and nail-technique and she has published a scholarly account of the last gatherings of harpers in Belfast in 1792. Her research and performances have greatly advanced our knowledge of the 17th and 18th century harpers and the music they played.

COLLECTORS

BUNTING, EDWARD (1773-1843)
Born in Armagh. While employed as organist in Belfast, he attended the final meeting of Irish harpers in 1792 and recorded their music as played. He then travelled around Ireland, adding to his collection. He published volumes of the music in 1796, 1809 and 1841. The value of his collections lies in his presentation of tunes as actually performed by the harpers, rather than as vocal, violin or pipe versions, many of which were transmitted in a corrupt form. In this respect, his contribution surpasses that of Petrie and Joyce. He died in Dublin in obscurity, but is now widely recognized for his role in preserving a considerable corpus of music which might otherwise have been lost.

COFFEY, MOTHER M. ATTRACTA (-1920)
Mother Attracta Coffey, whose *Irish Harp Tutor* and *27 Studies* are incorporated in this book, was a member of the Irish Branch of the Institute of the Blessed Virgin Mary, commonly known as 'Loreto'. She died at Loreto Abbey, Rathfarnham, Dublin, on 6 October 1920. Mother Attracta was a distinguished musician and was well-known in Ireland and England as a harpist of great talent. She was zealous in her efforts to revive interest in the harp and, as a practical step towards this, she published a Tutor and Exercises and arranged traditional melodies. The melodies were also subsequently arranged for the piano in association with Mr Vincent of London. She was instrumental in having competitions for harp included in the syllabus of the Feis Ceoil. As Mistress of Music at Rathfarnham, Mother Attracta worked in conjunction with the best musicians of her time and under her direction the school attained a standard of music, instrumental and vocal, for which it became noted at home and abroad. Among her many distinguished pupils was Mother Alphonsus O'Connor who succeeded her and maintained the standard of music at Rathfarnham which has become a tradition.

FOX, MRS CHARLOTTE MILLIGAN (-1916)
A sister of the poetess Alice Milligan, Charlotte was a native of Co. Tyrone and was the first Honorary Secretary of the Irish Folk Song Society (founded in 1904). She was an enthusiastic and talented member of the Publication Committee, editing some of its publications. She compiled and edited *Annals of the Irish Harpers* in 1911 and was instrumental in locating very valuable collections of old Irish folk songs.

HARDEBEC, CARL (1869-1945)
Born in London of a German father and Welsh mother. Blind from birth, he was introduced to music at an early age. He submitted his first composition in Ireland to the Dublin Feis Ceoil in 1897, gaining first prize, and continued to send works until 1908. He became interested in the movement to preserve Irish music and studied the collections of

Bunting, Petrie and Joyce. In 1900, at a Gaelic League concert in Belfast, he heard unaccompanied singing in Irish by a native speaker. The experience changed his perception of Irish music and he henceforth concentrated his efforts on studying and cultivating this aspect of the tradition. He studied the Irish language and poetry and, while in the Donegal Gaeltacht, transcribed on his Braille frame many traditional airs from the singers. He eventually invented a Braille alphabet in Irish for himself, which was later adopted by the National Institute for the Blind.

HARTY, SIR HERBERT HAMILTON (1879-1941)
Born in County Down. At the age of twelve he became a church organist, beginning as assistant to his father and progressing to posts in Belfast and Dublin. He was appointed to the Hallé Orchestra, Manchester, in 1920, and during the dozen or more years he retained the position he helped the orchestra to sustain the high reputation it had acquired under its founder and under Hans Richter and others. He later conducted in the United States and in Australia. He was particularly interested in the orchestral and choral work of Berlioz. As a composer he produced choral and orchestral works at festivals, concerts, etc. He was knighted in 1925 and was honorary D.Mus. of Dublin and Manchester and LL.D. of Belfast.

HUGHES, HERBERT (1882-1937)
Born in Belfast he was educated at the Royal College of Music. He occupied important positons as a music critic and helped to found the Irish Folk Song Society. He published a number of settings of Irish folk songs, as well as light-hearted original songs (sometimes humorous) that have gained popularity. He died in Brighton in 1937.

LARCHET, JOHN FRANCIS (1884-1967)
Born in Dublin. Studied at RIAM under M. Esposito. Mus.D. (TCD), FRIAM. Senior Vice-President and Professor of RIAM (1920 to 1955). Music Advisor to Irish Army, 1923). Director of Music, Abbey Theatre (1907 to 1934). Chair of Music UCD (1921 to 1958). Conductor of Dublin Amateur Orchestral Society. Director of Music Examinations in secondary schools. Vice-President, Trinity College of Music, London. President, Dublin Grand Opera Society. Hon. D.Mus. (NUI) 1953. Director of Concert and Assembly Hall Ltd. President, Irish Musical Fund. Decorated with Order of Commendatore of the Italian Republic, 1958. Irish traditional music was a source for many of his works, and as a teacher he was influential in developing a school of Irish composers. Died 1967.

O'SULLIVAN, DONAL (1893-1973) MA, Litt.D.
An authority on the subject of Irish music, on which he lectured and broadcast extensively. He was Director of Studies in Irish Folk Music and Song at University College, Dublin, as well as Lecturer in International Affairs at TCD. Among his publications are his edition in six volumes of the *Bunting Manuscripts* (1958) and his two-volume work entitled *O'Carolan – The Life, Times and Music of an Irish Harper*. He also contributed a number of articles relating to Irish traditional music to the Fifth Edition of *Grove's Dictionary of Music and Musicians* (edited by Eric Blom). A former member of the Irish Seanad, he numbered among his other activities membership of the Executive Board of the International Folk Music Council and of the Irish Council of the European Movement, of which he was President.

PETRIE, GEORGE (1789-1866)
Born in Dublin. He was an eminent painter and antiquary as well as an amateur violinist. He devoted his life to the collection of Irish folk tunes, and his work remains of fundamental importance for the study of Irish music. His complete collection has been republished, partly under the editorship of Stanford. The well-known Irish melody 'The Derry Air' was first found in print in the collection of 1855, where it appears with the indication that the name of the composer is unknown. It was given to Petrie by a Miss Jane Ross of Limavady. He died in Dublin.

STANFORD, CHARLES VILLIERS (1852-1924)
Born in Dublin. His father, a Dublin legal official, was a keen amateur musician, and he himself showed early musical gifts. His first composition was a march which he composed at the age of eight and which two or three years later was included in a pantomime at the Dublin Theatre Royal. At eighteen he went to Cambridge (MA, D.Mus.) where, at twenty-one, he became organist of Trinity College. He later became conductor of the University Musical Society. The Society gave many notable first British performances under his direction, especially of the works of Brahms, whom he greatly admired. At the age of twenty-four, at Tennyson's request, he wrote the music for the production of 'Queen Mary' at the Lyceum Theatre. He set a new standard in Anglican Church Music and exercised influence as Choral conductor, author, collector and editor of Irish folk tunes and, in particular, as a teacher at the Royal College of Music. For nearly forty years he was Professor of Music at his old university, and in 1901 he was knighted. The flavour of Irish folk tune sometimes showed itself in his work, and his list of compositions includes six Irish rhapsodies, an Irish symphony, and an Irish opera 'Shamus O'Brien'.

CONTEMPORARY COMPOSERS

BODLEY, SEÓIRSE, D.Mus.
Born Dublin 1933. Influences on his music range from the European avant-garde to Irish traditional music. His works include five symphonies for full orchestra, two chamber symphonies and numerous orchestral, choral, vocal and chamber pieces. Commissions include his Third Symphony, for the opening of the National Concert Hall in Dublin, and his Fourth, commissioned by the Arturo Toscanini Symphony Orchestra, Parma, Italy. Awards include the Arts Council Prize for Composition, a Travelling Studentship of the NUI, the Macauley Fellowship in Music Composition and the Marten Toonder Award. He is founder-member of Aosdána, Ireland's academy of creative artists.

BOYDELL, BRIAN (1917-2000)
Born in Dublin. Studied under Patrick Hadley, Herbert Howells and J.F. Larchet. LRIAM (singing), D.Mus. TCD, 1939. He was appointed Professor of Music, TCD (1962-82). Director, Dowland Consort. Council founder-member of Music Association of Ireland. An authority on music in eighteenth century Dublin, he was one of the most significant Irish musicians of his time. His compositional output was vast and he wrote a number of pieces for Irish harp. *A Pack of Fancies for a Travelling Harper* (1990) for solo harp is of particular interest.

DEALE, EDGAR M. (1902-1999)
Born in Dublin. Involved in choral singing all his life, specializing in the setting of voices. A founder-member of the Music Association of Ireland, he was editor of its first published catalogue of Twentieth-Century Irish Music. He was a Director of Concert and Assembly Hall Ltd and a Governor of the RIAM. He had been President and longest serving member of the Culwick Choral Society, the oldest established Choir in Dublin.

FLEISCHMANN, ALOYS (1910-1992) MA, BMus. (UCC)
Studied composition and conducting at State Academy of Music, Munich and musicology at Munich University, 1932-34. Appointed Professor of Music at UCC, 1934. D. Mus. (NUI) 1963 and Hon. Mus.D. (TCD) 1964. Founder and conductor of Cork Symphony Orchestra and Chairman of Cork Orchestral Society. Chairman, organizing committee of Cork International Choral Festival. He served on the Advisory Committee for Cultural Relations and was a member of the Irish National Commission for UNESCO. Contributor of articles to *Grove's Dictionary* and the *Encyclopaedia Americana* and to various journals. Wrote many major works. His final great research project, *Sources of Irish Traditional Music: 1600-1855*, was completed shortly before his death.

FRIEL, JAMES REDMOND (1907-1980)
Headmaster of Waterside Boys School, Derry. Studied music privately with Dr Norman Hay, organist of St Columbus Church, Derry. Member of the music staff of St Columb's College and a member of the Arts Council of Northern Ireland. He was a founder-member of the North West Music Society and of the North West Arts Festival. Acted as adjudicator at Feiseanna and as music assessor in BBC Belfast.

KELLY, THOMAS C. (1917-1985)
Studied music in National University of Ireland (BMus.) Music Master at Clongowes Wood College. Influenced by Irish folk music and Anglo-Irish composers such as Stanford, Harty and Hughes. He was the first to write a work for Irish harp and small orchestra.

KINSELLA, JOHN
Born in Dublin. Self-taught as a composer but has always devoted a considerable amount of time to chamber music playing. He was head of music in RTÉ from 1983-88 and since taking early retirement has devoted himself to composition, writing some large-scale works, including symphonies and concertos.

MCNULTY, DANIEL (1920-1996) BMus. (NUI), FRCO (London), LRIAM.
Organist and Choirmaster, Augustinian Church, Thomas Street, Dublin. Awarded prizes for composition at Feis Ceoil and the Oireachtas. He wrote orchestral, instrumental and much sacred music, of which the masses are probably the best known, being sung in many churches at Sunday worship.

NELSON, HAVELOCK (1917-1996)
Born in Cork. Educated in Dublin. MA, MSc., PhD., D.Mus. (TCD), LRAM. Co-founder of the Dublin Orchestral Players with Constance Harding (1939). Member of music staff of BBC Northern Ireland as accompanist and conductor. Founder and conductor of Studio Symphony Orchestra, also conductor of Ulster Singers. Director and conductor of Studio Opera Group, which many years later provided the inspiration for the Castleward Opera. Examiner in music and adjudicator. Also contributed musical articles to various journals. Awarded an OBE (1966) for distinguished services to music.

Ó hÉIGEARTAIGH, CIAN
Born 1944. Son of Seán Ó hÉigeartaigh. Publisher in Irish language. Studied composition in RIAM under Dr A.J. Potter. Prizewinner at various Feiseanna and Oireachtas. Particularly interested in composition of Irish traditional music. Currently working as journalist.

Ó GALLHOBHAIR, ÉAMONN (1906-1983)
Born in Dundalk. Studied at Leinster School of Music and RIAM. Became interested in Irish music and joined and performed at An Ceol Cumann, 1930, through which he initiated broadcasts of music from Radio Éireann, particularly Chamber Music. Active as an adjudicator and in Feis Átha Cliath, for which he wrote test pieces. Active also as a critic and editor. Assistant Music Director, Radio Éireann and Director of the (then) RÉ light Orchestra. Was for some years Music Consultant to the Abbey Theatre in Dublin. He composed an opera 'Nocturne sa gCearnóg' and some pieces for solo Irish harp. He lived in Spain following his retirement and died there.

POTTER, A. J. (1918-1980)
Born in Belfast. Studied at the RCM London with Vaughan Williams, R.G. Morris and H.C. Colles. Won the Radio Éireann O'Carolan Prize for Composition (1952 and 1953). Mus.D TCD (1953). Professor of Composition at RIAM (1952-73). Composed several works especially for the (then) Radio Éireann Light Orchestra and, at the request of Cairde na Cruite, *Teach lán le Cruitirí* for nine Irish harps and concert harp.

TRIMBLE, JOAN (1915-2000)
Born in Enniskillen, Co Fermanagh. Educated Enniskillen and TCD. BA (TCD), Mus.B. Studied violin and piano with her mother and later at RIAM, Dublin, with J.F. Larchet, Claud Biggs, Annie Lord and Ferrucio Grossi. Studied at RCM, London. Piano with Arthur Benjamin and composition with Herbert Howells and Ralph Vaughan Williams. Won many prizes for composition and wrote commissioned works for the BBC, including an opera for television entitled 'Blind Raftery'. Was partner with her sister Valerie in their highly successful and famous duo for two pianos. She was conferred with an honorary fellowship from the RIAM in 1985 and also received an honorary degree from Queen's University Belfast.

VICTORY, GERARD (1921-1995)
Born in Dublin. Graduated from UCD in Celtic Studies and Modern Languages and from TCD in Music. Worked as producer on RTÉ sound radio and television. Director of music RTÉ 1967-82. One of the organizers of the Dublin Festival of Twentieth-Century Music. He composed more than 200 works, including a harp concerto.

WILSON, JAMES
Born in London. Studied piano, harpsichord, violin, clarinet and composition under Alex Rowley. Has specialised in the study of the folk music of Europe and Central America. Living in Dublin since 1948, he has made a most significant contribution to the music scene in Ireland. A prolific composer, he was Professor of Composition at the RIAM and a director of the Ennis/IMRO Composition Summer School. He is particularly interested in writing for strings and in vocal music, especially in opera. He works frequently in Denmark. He has written a sonata for harp.

THE AUTHOR

SHEILA LARCHET CUTHBERT
Received her early musical education from her parents, both eminent musicians, and later at the Royal Irish Academy of Music where she studied piano and cello. Prizewinner at Feis Ceoil in both instruments. Commenced harp study with the late Mother Alphonsus O'Connor at Loreto Abbey, Rathfarnham, Dublin, and continued with the eminent French harpist, Tina Bonifacio. Obtained Degree of BMus. at UCD. Held several important orchestral positions: Principal Harpist in the Liverpool Philharmonic Orchestra, the Hallé Orchestra in Manchester and the (then) RTÉSO in Dublin. Member of the Prieur Instrumental Ensemble. Established class for Irish and concert harp in the College of Music. Took part in series of Radio Éireann programmes presented by Dr Donal O'Sullivan, entitled 'Songs of the Irish', making many arrangements of music of O'Carolan and the pre-O'Carolan harpers. Represents Ireland on the Corporation and Board of Directors of the World Harp Congress.

ACKNOWLEDGEMENTS

Mother Attracta Coffey, *Tutor For The Irish Harp*, and *27 Studies* (Exercises and Studies throughout) — Loreto Abbey, Rathfarnham, Dublin

Dr Donal O'Sullivan, *O'Carolan: The Life, Time and Music of an Irish Harper*, vol. 2 (and all O'Carolan compositions) — Routledge and Kegan Paul, London
Also words of 'The Small Black Rose' from *Songs of the Irish* — Browne & Nolan Ltd., Dublin
Also: *The Irish Folk Song Society Journal*

Songs of the Irish Harpers by C. Milligan Fox (Air – 'The Parting of Friends' - Lesson II) — Bayley and Ferguson, London

Percy A. Scholes, *The Oxford Companion to Music* (Data throughout) — Oxford University Press

Edward Bunting (Collections) (Mercedes Bolger (Garvey) – Lesson IV) — 1796, 1809 and 1840

George Petrie (Collection) (Mercedes McGrath (Bolger) - Lesson V)

The Fitzwilliam Virginal Book ('The Irish Ho-hone' – Lesson III)

A Catalogue of Contemporary Irish Composers (Data for biographies) — The Music Association of Ireland

Encyclopaedia of Ireland — Figgis, Dublin

Joan Rimmer, *The Irish Harp* (Historical data) — The Mercier Press: Cork and Dublin

'Cairde na Cruite' is indebted to the following subscribers whose generosity made the publication of this book possible:

An Chomhairle Ealaíon
An tOireachtas
Sighle Bairéad, Baile Átha Cliath
Mrs Mercedes Bolger, Gorey
Eibhlín Ní Chathailriabhaigh, Baile Átha Cliath
Nuala Bean Uí Cholgáin
The Convent of Mercy, Moate
Cumann Lúthchleas Ghael
Lil Nic Dhonncha, Baile Átha Cliath
Mrs Mercedes Garvey, Baile Átha Cliath
Miss Kathleen H. Goodfellow, Baile Átha Cliath
A. Guinness Son & Co. Ltd, Baile Átha Cliath
Mrs Bonnie Hyndeman, California
Mr Victor Jackson, Baile Átha Cliath
Loreto Abbey, Rathfarnham
Lord Moyne, Castleknock
McCullough/Pigott Ltd, Suffolk Street, Dublin 2
New Ireland Assurance Co. Ltd
Mrs Leone Poulson, New Jersey
Máirin Ní Shé (Bean Mhicheál Feiritéir) Corca Dhuibhne, Dún Droma
Gráinne agus Micheál Yeats, Baile Átha Cliath
Micheál Ó hUanacháin
Bord na Gaeilge
Conradh na Gaeilge
Susan Langley Trust
Members of Cairde na Cruite